I'm not trying to pick a fight. I'm really not.

I know the content, themes, and ideas in this book are potentially going to generate some kind of negative reaction and push-back in some people, because they either think that they have had some really great life advice in the past, or they think they give great advice and that there's nothing wrong with doing that.

My advice (ironically) to you: have an open mind and see if I can get you to think differently about advice.

Do you really need it?

Should you take it from everyone?

Or can I encourage you to back yourself a bit more?

For more from Nick Bowditch, including his other books, the best-selling *Reboot Your Thinking* and its follow-up book, *Actually, it IS all about me*, as well as information on booking Nick to speak at your event, and therapy resources and bookings, please go to nickbowditch.com.

Your advice sucks.

How to stop *giving* advice.

And how to stop *asking for it*.

First published in 2022 by Nick Bowditch
© Nick Bowditch 2022
The moral rights of the author have been asserted.

All inquiries should be made to the author.
ISBN: 9780995408333
A catalogue entry is available for this book from the National Library of Australia.
Cover design by Nick Bowditch.

Disclaimer: The material in this publication is of the nature of general comment only, and does not represent professional advice. It is not intended to provide specific guidance for particular circumstances and it should not be relied on as the basis for any decision to take action or not take action on any matter which it covers. Readers should obtain professional advice where appropriate, before making any such decision. To the maximum extent permitted by law, the author and publisher disclaim all responsibility and liability to any person, arising directly or indirectly from any person taking or not taking action based on the information in this publication.

Acknowledgements:

My kids are such an inspiration to me and such a reason for me to always try to be better.

I am so proud of them.

I am so proud to be their Dad.

And they just make me feel prouder of myself.

I love them so much.

My Mum and Dad weren't big advice givers, but they were, nonetheless, great teachers. I am so grateful for their lessons.

My great mates, Kyle Reed and Pedro Gomes, who have been such a good sounding board and reflector for me since the start of my recovery, thank you.

To my own therapist, Ron Blanchard, the wisest, most sensible, and kindest bloke I know. I owe you more than you will ever really know mate.

One of my longest and oldest (ha!) friends, Marnie Dixon. You know everything. I hope you know what a gift to my life you have been.

To everyone who reads my books, listens to my podcasts, comes to hear me speak on stage, looks at my website, or has ever given me a little dopamine hit on social media, thank you.

And to four of my great teachers, Brenè Brown, Liz Gilbert, Malcolm Gladwell and the wonderful Andrew Griffiths: keep writing, and I'll keep reading.

To my beautiful, capable, intelligent,
and kind children, to whom I have given
so much advice, much of it probably rubbish.

Sorry about that.

CONTENTS

Introduction:
Anyone who gives you advice thinks you're an idiot.   18

The WMAG's   23

How to cure mental illness.   25

When is advice not advice?   31

Feedback is a gift.   32

What about criticism?   39

A book about how advice sucks that's full of advice?   43

A quick note about working your way through this book   44

Chapter 1:   46

Why do people ask for advice?

Lack of confidence.   49

Codependence.   51

Validation.   60

To have someone to blame.   78

Do they even want your advice?   85

Chapter 2:   89

Why do people give advice?

They think they are helping.   92

They think they know better.   95

They want to control someone.   98

They want to reduce their own anxiety.   100

They want to show how smart they are.   101

They are spelling correctors.   102

They have no power elsewhere in their life.   104

They can't see past their own rigidity.   107

They have to be right.   109

They think it's impressive.   110

They are suckers for nostalgia.   112

They literally can't help themselves.   114

They need to consolidate their 'better-than' (and your 'less-than') position.   115

They do it for themselves.   117

Chapter 3:   119

Why giving advice is a terrible idea.

You don't know the whole story.   122

You are in the way of growth.   124

You don't know what you don't know.   126

You have a difference experience to them.   129

You are not supporting them, you are   131
judging them.

You are probably just telling them what   133
they want to hear.

You are just telling them what most other   136
people will tell them anyway.

It gets you entwined.   139

You don't have to deal with the fallout.   140

We are much better at being sympathetic   142
when someone loses than being happy
when someone wins.

Which advice have you actually   144
remembered? And why advice have you
actually taken?

But isn't therapy advice?   146

Chapter 4:   153

Some of the best advice I've ever been given.

Chapter 5:   157

Some of the suckiest advice ever given.

Follow your passion.   160

Never give up.   165

Be strong.   169

You are over-reacting.   172

Good things come to those who wait.   175

You are perfect just the way you are.   178

You can do anything you put your mind   180
to.

Success is a journey, not a destination.   183

Just be positive.   187

Fake it 'til you make it.   189

If you love what you do, you'll never work   192
a day in your life.

Stop playing the victim. 195

They are just being an attention-seeker. 198

Just say yes, and then work it out. 200

Patience is a virtue. 203

You are entitled to your opinion. 204

I'm living the dream. 207

That's impossible. 210

It is what it is. 212

Everything happens for a reason. 216

Chapter 6: 221

How to stop getting advice.

Boundaries people! 225

The polite decline. 227

The less-polite decline. 230

Back yourself. 232

Chapter 7: 237

How to stop giving advice.

Leave some space.   244

"I'm not giving advice, I'm giving information."   246

Understand your own motivation.   248

What do you need from me?   251

What do *you* think you should do?   254

I can tell you what *I* would do.   256

How can I help?   258

Chapter 8:   260

The start.

INTRODUCTION:

Anyone who gives you advice
thinks you're an idiot.

If you are someone who loves to give advice, you're probably not going to enjoy this book.

Oh, and if you are someone who regularly asks other people for their advice? Well, you might not be a fan of mine after a few chapters of this either.

See, I think advice is largely a self-serving, narcissistic, arrogant misbehaviour that, if we really thought about it, most of us wouldn't think of giving to anyone else in a million years.

Also, anyone who gives you advice thinks you're an idiot.

Read that again, and tell me I'm wrong.

Nobody is offering advice to someone they think is smarter than them, or wiser than them, or more experienced or more successful or more powerful than them, are they?

Advice is usually given down, not up.

It's a symptom of a power imbalance between two people.

It's mean, and judgemental, and self-righteous.

I reckon in about nine times out of ten, advice was neither asked for, needed, or wanted. Yet, it was given anyway.

We just can't help ourselves.

We need to be the one with the most-sage counsel. The *one* person who knows the magic remedy that nobody else does. The one who saved them when *everyone else* was unable to.

I know this because it used to be me.

I was the most judgemental and self-righteous person ever.

I couldn't wait to give you advice on your life, or on the behaviour of your children, or on your relationship.

This was all obviously before my own life was examined, I had my own children, and my marriage ended.

There is something particularly and sensationally arrogant about giving people parental advice before you have had any children of your own.

But there I was.

Fast forward through years of therapy, a couple of stints in rehab, four beautiful yet imperfect children (like everyone's), a crappy divorce, and getting qualified as a therapist and offering trauma therapy to loads of other imperfect people, and I am a very different person today.

To a point.

My battle to not be so judgey and self-righteous is a constant one.

Not with my therapy clients, that's easy.

I know my job there is to mostly just listen and help them find their own answers in a safe and supportive space.

But outside of that, I still want to tell my friends and family what they are doing wrong, and how much better they could do it if they just listened to me and took my advice!

Ironic, huh?

I'm not saying that everyone who offers someone advice is some kind of ego-driven megalomaniac monster.

Not all of them ...

———————————— · ————————————

The WMAG's.

The Well-Meaning Advice-Giver, or WMAG as I like to call them, thinks they are helping.

They think that they are genuinely providing a solution for someone out of kindness and altruism. They mean well. Right?

We are so conditioned from when we are young, to share and to help and to be there for someone else who needs us, that we can't shake that practice as we grow into adulthood.

The majority of us are people-pleasers.

We are mostly so hopelessly codependent that we can't even hear someone say they are struggling a bit, or that they are slightly unsure of what to do, without sticking our noses in and telling them what *we* think they should do.

And the majority of these people-pleasers are absolutely WMAG's.

Most of them have very little control over, or power in, their own lives.

They don't want to see you make the same mistakes they have made and end up with the lives they have ended up with.

They so desperately want to escape their own lives, but can't.

So, they make it their mission not to let anyone else experience any sadness or frustration in theirs.

You know these people, I guarantee it.

And the great irony of these WMAG's is they are saying constructive and potentially helpful things. But when you ask them why they haven't followed their own advice, they can only shrug.

It's much easier to instruct someone else into a good life than to face their own challenges head on and change *their* life.

It's much easier to support you and try to make *you* happy, then to deal with their own unhappiness.

————————————— . —————————————

How to cure mental illness.

If you've read my other books, *Reboot Your Thinking* and *Actually, it IS all about me*, you will already know that my mind works a bit different to other people.

I have lived with mental ill-health for a long time, on and off, and in varying degrees of messiness.

And when you both live with mental ill-health AND talk about it on stage and write about it in books, you get a lot of advice about how to live with it, survive it, even cure it!

And I mean a *lot*.

"You have to see my therapist, she is amazing."

OK, well I am on my fourth long-term therapist now. It has taken me a long time to get to them, and I have had to talk about my traumatic shit over and over and over again to loads of strangers to get this far.

I am unlikely to do it again right now with your therapist.

Also, what makes you think that (a) my therapist isn't world-class already, (b) your therapist is for some reason going to be better, and importantly, (c) I was asking you for a recommendation?

"You need to micro-dose psychedelics; they have cured my brother's friend's mental illness completely:"

OK, but there is a chance that my mental health and your randomly-obscure acquaintance's mental health, are not the same, and therefore might not need the same kind of therapeutic intervention.

Although the psychedelic part sounds kind of fun.

After the 7th person offers this advice though, I'm usually favouring a macro, as opposed to micro, dosing option.

"You need to burn [insert any one of hundreds of essential oils here] in your home. If you don't have any of them, I can sell you some. And a burner too!"

How handy that this helpful friend knows the exact aromatherapy solution for my malaise that she has only just heard about AND she just happens to sell that particular oil as her side-hustle. What are the odds?

"Just be less anxious".

"What do you have to be sad about?".

"There is always something worse off you know".

Or my all-time favourite: "Just choose not to be depressed. Happiness is a choice!"

Punching someone in the throat for saying ridiculous and unhelpful things when you are feeling at your very worst is a choice too.

I have had people tell me that my mental ill-health is basically imaginary on my part ("it's all in your head"), totally curable, not as bad as theirs, and just something that everybody has to deal with.

It's all in my head? Thanks Kylie, yes, it is.

Ignoring for a moment the fact that you just told me that what I am experiencing isn't real, that I am basically mad as a hatter for believing it, and seemingly fixable if I just stop believing it, you are actually right.

My mental illness *is* in my head.

And that's the part that makes it just a little bit more shit than some other chronic illnesses.

If I had a bone or muscle condition that affected my movement it would be obvious to the world when they saw me.

If I had asthma, I would use an inhaler quite proudly and in public without anyone telling me I am doing it wrong, or that my asthma doesn't actually exist.

If I had cancer, nobody would be telling me to just get over it, and that it was all in my head.

But *my* chronic illness *is* in my head. It's invisible. And it affects everybody differently.

But I'm not imagining it. It's not unreal, no matter how much I wish it was.

As a therapist, I often hear people's stories and life-experiences that are really dreadful. Sad and harrowing and heavy. I often think how damaging it would be for some of my clients to tell someone, even a small part of their stories, and be met with something like the above.

After years of working with people in a one-on-one therapeutic environment and hearing lots of these terrible stories, I have found – by far – the most effective and caring response is usually something like: "Wow, that sounds really shit".

My clients invariably look relieved if anything, and then say something like "yes, it *is* shit, thanks for nor trying to fix that straight away or tell me what I should do".

A client once disclosed some terrible abuse they experienced as a child at the hands of their grandparents.

Their mother's mother and father tormented and abused her from when she was very little, until the age where she finally found the courage to put a stop to it.

The abuse was mostly emotional, but was also physical, and in some terrible instances, it was sexual.

When she eventually told their mother what had been going on for years, she didn't believe her. She never spoke of it again, until she were sitting opposite me in a therapy session, and it all came tumbling out.

The whole time she was telling me this terrible story, I could see that she really wanted me to make sense of it.

To tell her what to do. What to feel. What to say.

But that's not how therapy works.

Sometimes, though, you can meet people where they are. And you can support them in what you say, without giving any advice or telling them what to do.

"So yeah, that's what happened", she said.

"That is terrible", I said.

She looked relieved, as if she was waiting for me to either discount her feelings or worse, as her mum had done, not believed her.

And then the clincher: "Mum could have believed me. She could have asked me more about it. She could have confronted them."

My simple reply: "Yep".

"What do you think of my grandparents now that you know that", she asked, again waiting for me to dilute her experience by saying something trite like they didn't realise what they were doing, or it was just their way, or it was a different time.

"I think they are fucking monsters", I said, because it's true.

The client was obviously taken back, but then in an instant I could see a wave of relief wash over her, a recognition that she was finally not alone in this nightmare, and that her feelings mattered.

It wasn't my place – or the right time – for me to tell her what to do or to encourage her to confront her mum or her grandparents.

My place was to simply hold her space.

To be *with*.

Words have power. I think that *should* and *must* and *need to* are perilously unhelpful in most sentences.

These kinds of words are the fuel of advice. In fact, it's very difficult to give advice without using those words.

Want to steer clear of giving advice?

Steer clear of *should* and *must* and *need to*.

When is advice not advice?

Three things that look much the same on the surface, but are actually miles apart, are feedback, criticism, and advice.

Feedback is defined as "information about reactions to a product, a person's performance of a task, etc. which is used as a basis for improvement"[1].

Criticism is "the expression of disapproval of someone or something on the basis of perceived faults or mistakes"[2].

And advice is defined as "guidance or recommendations offered with regard to prudent future action"[3].

All three of them require one person (the receiver), to be of a lower station than the other (the giver), because they (the receiver) require improvement, have perceived faults or mistakes, or they need to take more prudent action in the future.

But are they all a negative thing?

---

[1] Oxford English Dictionary
[2] Oxford English Dictionary
[3] Lexico

Feedback is a gift.

I think feedback, actually, is a gift.

And I don't think feedback and advice are the same thing.

I can receive feedback on my job performance, on my cooking, or on my ability to speak on stage at a conference in front of thousands of people, and I can benefit from that feedback.

I can be better because of it.

But I don't accept feedback from everybody. In fact, I accept feedback from very few people.

For instance, when I speak on stage in front of an audience, often that audience is – for some reason – asked to provide feedback on me and the other speakers who were on stage that day.

When presented with this feedback, I look through it, pulling out the feedback from other professional speakers, or the other people who spoke on stage at that event, and promptly file the rest of it in the bin.

I'm not listening to Wendy or Kevin's feedback about my speaking ability when they have just happened to come to that event that day, might never come to another event, or have been to one before, and have never stood on stage in front of a thousand people and shared their story.

Why would I?

And why would you?

Part of my brand is that when I speak on stage at conferences, regardless of how buttoned-down and corporate the gig is, I always wear the same thing: jeans, a plain black t-shirt, and thongs (flip-flops if you are reading this in a part of the world where the word thong just made you either giggle or become uncomfortable).

On more than one occasion, I have received the 'feedback' that I should dress differently when I speak on stage. Pointedly, I have never received this feedback from another professional speaker, only ever anonymously from someone sitting in the cheap seats.

Once though, the feedback was delivered straight to me after a speaking gig, as I was signing some copies of my book that the delegates were receiving as part of their showbag from the event.

"Can I give you some advice?", a lady asked me as I signed her copy.

I looked up and smiled. "If you like", I said.

"I think your talk was great, and the stuff you said was all good and helpful, but … ", here we go I thought, "if you want people to take you seriously, you should wear shoes on stage".

Just think about that for a second.

The amazing confidence someone has to have to come up to someone who is doing THEIR JOB, a job that they don't do and probably can't do, and telling them that they, in fact, can't do their job unless they do it the way they are telling them to. That I should wear what *they* are telling me to wear, rather than what I want to, or what I feel comfortable in, or what is part of my brand.

Also, "if people want to take me seriously"? Translation: "I don't take you seriously". I mean it's one thing to think that, but entirely something else to say to someone. Point blank. To their face!

Now, I would love to tell you I went into a huge, well-rehearsed rant with this lady about my brand, and my comfort, and the fact that I do take what I do and say on stage very seriously. Or asked her what the actual fuck difference me having shoes on or not would possibly make to that.

I would love to tell you that I replied, "Oh, really? Is that what *you* wear when *you* are delivering keynote presentations on stage at conferences?".

But I didn't.

I just smiled, and said "thanks".

I have to pick my battles. There was about one thousand other people in the room that day, and she was the only person who told me I should have shoes on.

999 other people either didn't care, or received my message without being distracted by something as trivial as what I had on my feet, or agreed with her, but didn't feel compelled to give me – a complete stranger who didn't ask for it – her advice.

I'm always going to focus my energy on the 999. That's a great metaphor for my life I reckon.

If another author wanted to give me some feedback on my books, if another therapist wanted to give me some feedback about my work, or if another parent – of children *just like mine* – wanted to give me some feedback on my parenting, I would be a mug not to listen.

But if you've never written anything and then been vulnerable enough to share it with the world, or if you have never provided therapy for anyone in a professional environment, or if you have no kids? Then sorry, you might think you are entitled to your opinions, but that doesn't mean I have to be entitled to your feedback.

As the great Brenè Brown[4] wrote: "If you are not in the arena getting your ass kicked on occasion, I am

---

[4] @brenebrown

not interested in or open to your feedback. There are a million cheap seats in the world today filled with people who will never be brave with their own lives, but will spend every ounce of energy they have hurling advice and judgement at those of us trying to dare greatly. Their only contributions are criticism, cynicism, and fear-mongering. If you're criticizing from a place where you're not also putting yourself on the line, I'm not interested in your feedback."

I'm with you Brenè. As usual.

The loudest boos come from the cheapest seats, and I am done with letting people who are covering their own fear, attack me for investigating my own curiosity.

Get in the arena, or shhh.

Brown also created a checklist of eleven things that improve the space in which feedback is both given and received.

She wrote that feedback is best given when you are ready to sit next to the person you are giving feedback to, as opposed to across from them, and when you are ready to put the problem in front of both of you, rather than between you.

How simple, but great, is that?

How often have you received feedback from a boss across a big desk where they are on one side, and you are on the other?

And how receptive to that feedback were you?

Brown stresses the importance of the feedback-giver being ready to listen and ask questions instead of just giving their opinion, and acknowledging what the other person is good at or has done well, including how they might use these personal strengths in this particular situation.

She notes the importance of giving feedback without using shame or blaming the other person, and says the feedback-giver should be able to accept their own role in the situation they are discussing, showing gratitude for the other person, and being open enough to match the vulnerability of the person receiving the feedback[5].

How often have you received feedback from someone when all of those parameters were met?

My guess is not often.

And my guess is also that if the person giving the feedback did meet all of those criteria, you would have absolutely taken their feedback on board.

---

[5] The PDF of the checklist is available at https://daretolead.brenebrown.com/

The loudest boos come from the cheapest seats.

What about criticism?

Criticism doesn't always have to be a negative thing.

I think the important distinction with criticism is how prescriptively it's given.

I mean, if I was a commercial airline pilot, and when landing at Sydney Airport I performed a pretty messy and bouncy and rough landing, and then another, more experienced pilot who was a passenger on that flight, mentioned a very prescriptive piece of criticism to help me land in Sydney better next time, I'm taking that criticism all day long.

But if a parent is just on their kid's back all day, every day, about their grades, and their friends, and their chores, and telling them that they are rubbish, and constantly criticising them in a demeaning and belittling way, without ever mentioning something good or positive or uplifting, then they are not being helpful and are frankly, kind of a jerk.

Advice, on the other hand, has little, if any, redeeming features.

And when someone can magically combine advice *and* criticism, it turns into a really toxic cocktail.

That kind of advice reduces the focus of both the advice-giver and the advice-receiver to what is wrong, and bad, instead of the possibility of what could be.

People are not their mistakes, and we rarely have only one label hanging around our necks.

Criticism as advice increases blame and there is very little that is constructive coming out of any of that.

And, if you needed any more reasons not to use criticism as advice: it doesn't work!

Dr. Steven Stosny[6] wrote that criticism fails because it embodies two of the things that human beings hate the most:

1. It calls for submission, and we hate to submit.
2. It devalues, and we hate to feel devalued.

"While people hate to submit", Stosny wrote, "we actually like to cooperate.

Critical people seem oblivious to this key point about human nature.

The valued self cooperates, the devalued self resists. If you want behavior change from a partner, child, relative, or friend, first show value for the person. If you want resistance, criticize."

So why, if we are smart enough to realise that being critical in advice doesn't work, do we do it anyway?

---

[6] https://www.amazon.com/Steven-Stosny/

"It's because criticism is an easy form of ego defence", Stonsy says. "We don't criticize because we *disagree* with a behavior or an attitude.

We criticize because we somehow feel devalued by the behaviour or attitude. Critical people tend to be easily insulted and especially in need of ego defence.

Critical people were often criticized in early childhood by caretakers, siblings, or peers, at an age when criticism can be especially painful.

They cannot distinguish criticism of their behavior from outright rejection, no matter how much we try to make the distinction for them, as in the well-intentioned, "You're a good boy, but this behavior is bad."

Such a distinction requires a higher prefrontal cortex operation, which is beyond most young children. For a child under seven, anything more than occasional criticism, even if soft-pedalled, means they're bad and unworthy."[7]

Little surprise that they often then grow into adults who are not only big on giving advice, but use criticism to do it.

---

[7] Stosny. (1995). Treating attachment abuse: a compassionate approach. Springer Pub. Company.

Friendship will not stand the strain of very much good advice for very long.

Robert Staughton Land

A book about why advice sucks that's full of advice?

As we work through this book, I will delve deeper into why people ask for advice, why people give it, and why giving advice is a terrible idea. I will detail some of the suckiest advice that people give. And then finally talk about how to stop getting - and giving - advice.

And I get it by the way. "Hang on", you might be thinking, "so this is a book that gives advice about why giving advice is a bad idea?"

And yes. It is. To that, I will give you three quotes:

"Inconsistency is the only thing in which men are consistent."[8]

"Consistency is the hobgoblin of little minds."[9]

And "Inconsistencies in men are generally testimony to their immaturity."[10]

You can choose whichever suits you best.

You don't need my advice.

---

[8] Credit: Horace Smith
[9] Credit: My boy, Ralph Waldo Emerson
[10] Credit: Edwin Louis Cole

A quick note about working your way through this book.

I have tried to keep the chapters pretty clear and used a heap of headings to make skimming through the book easier.

Or, if you just pick it up and read five minute's worth it should make more sense too.

You might have already noticed that I have also included some footnotes with quick explanations or links at the bottom of the page that the reference is on.

I have tried to include many and all references to other people's work that I talk about in the book, so that you can check out their great work and expand your thinking a bit more with their ideas too.

Some contributors are famous and well-known, and some are just favourites of mine that you might not have come across yet.

Either way, I hope it all makes sense.

Dive in with an open mind.

I hope you enjoy it.

CHAPTER 1:

Why do people ask for advice?

If advice is such a toxic and terrible thing, why do so many of us still ask for it?

What makes us seek out someone to either validate what we already know to be true, or tell us what they think is the best course of action?

Even though they sometimes know very little about us, and probably even less about the situation, the people involved, and all of the other intricate nuances you haven't – and probably won't – even tell them?

Are you so insecure and lacking in confidence that you can't make even the simplest of decisions in your life by yourself, and without support or acknowledgement from someone else?

Well ... actually, that is one of the biggest reasons we ask someone else for advice.

Lack of confidence.

There are thousands of reasons why people lack confidence in themselves.

While some of them are genetic in origin, the majority of these reasons stem from how someone else has treated us – or mistreated us – in our lives, most notably in our childhood.

Dr. Barbara Markway[11] wrote that two important happiness chemicals in our brains, Serotonin and Oxytocin, can be limited by some people's genes and not others, therefore affecting their level of self-confidence well beyond their own control[12].

But our self-confidence is much more likely to be messed with by other people, and the life experiences; trauma; bullying; parenting styles; and sexual, gender-based, or racial discrimination that they can bring into people's lives over an extended period of time.

This makes it even more astounding that so many of us find the answer to dealing with this lack of esteem and confidence, being to seek approval and validation from someone else.

Even when that person is the *same* person who caused you that trauma in the first place!

---

[11] @barbmarkway

[12] Markway, B., Ampel, C. (2018). The Self Confidence Workbook. A Guide to Overcoming Self-Doubt and Improving Self-Esteem. Althea Press.

But we do seek it from them, and because of the nature of their personalities, they are more than happy to provide it.

Actually, the people who undermine our confidence and self-esteem are also the same people who are happy to provide advice, whether we ask for it or not.

A survey I created when researching this book, was answered by 3,122 people. It had just two questions: have you ever had a person in your life who has 'dramatically lowered your self-confidence and self-esteem'? And have you also received advice from that person, whether or not you asked for it?

The first, and sad, result was 2,779 of the 3,122 people who responded, had indeed had someone in their life who had messed with their self-esteem.

But here's the really interesting part: while nearly 80% of the respondents were given advice by the same person who had damaged their self-confidence, 72% of the respondents actually *asked* that person for advice!

Such is the damage that these kinds of people can inflict on us that they create a sort of Stockholm Syndrome where our tormentor becomes our advisor. How is a messed-up situation like that ever going to work in our favour?

---·---

Codependence.

Codependence is when someone prioritises the needs, desires, and outcomes of other people ahead of their own.

The best description of codependence I have heard, is that it's like asking somebody else how *you* feel.

One of the world's best experts on codependence is Pia Mellody. She explained that a codependent person has problems with self-esteem.

They have difficulty setting and holding boundaries, or owning their own reality.

They have difficulty even recognising that they have their own needs and wants, far less thinking they are as important as someone else's, and tend not to be able to feel any emotion strongly or appropriately until someone they are interdependent with, is feeling that emotion properly first.

Codependence is really common in relationships and families that exist alongside active addiction, unresolved trauma, and dysregulated emotions.

But how does that relate to giving or getting advice?

Well, because codependent people have problems with boundaries, emotions, communication of needs, trust, and self-confidence and valuing themselves, they also have problems with advice, either seeking it too often or unnecessarily, or giving it unsolicited and annoyingly.

Scenario 1: the codependent person seeking positive reinforcement from their partner.

"What do you think of this new outfit?"

"I dunno, it looks OK", their partner replies, barely even looking.

"Just OK? Do you think it makes me look fat?"

"I dunno! What difference does it make what I think of it? It's *your* outfit."

[Unsaid]

"Because I really need you to validate me.

To validate my buying decision in the first place.

To convince me that it makes me more attractive to you.

That it's OK for me to like it and to like the way I feel in it.

To tell me *how* I feel in it.

To give me a sign that I might be enough … for the outfit, for this nice feeling I have in it, for you, for the world."

[Said]

"No, you're right, it doesn't matter", as they go and change into something their partner has said they *did* like once before.

They are asking the other person how they feel.

And it might seem like an extreme example, but in codependent relationships, this exchange is happening hundreds of times in one hundred different ways, about one hundred different topics.

Scenario 2: the codependent person giving advice that nobody asked for.

Mum: "I don't think she is right for you."

Son: "Why not?"

[Unsaid]

Mum: "Because I am not finished being your mother yet.

Because your father ignores me and I want to squeeze every last bit of affection and attention out of you to make up for it while I still can.

Because she is going to love you in a way I never can, and you might choose that love over mine and forget me.

Because I don't want you to make any of the same mistakes I did in relationships, so best if you just don't have any, and stay with me for every minute of your life until I die."

[Said]

Mum: "I don't know exactly. She seems sneaky. She's not good enough for you. You can do better."

Oooohhh, that stings, don't it?

Codependence can sometimes manifest itself as an interest, even an obsession, with other people's problems, and your desire to solve those problems for them.

And for a lot of people, the solution just spills out of them, without ever even being asked for.

"Here's my opportunity, while you are really ill and weak and looking terrible, to finally establish some superiority over you and make myself feel worthwhile and important" can sound like "Here's the number of a physician that I know personally who can definitely help you. I've called him and he knows all about you and is waiting to help".

The even suckier side of codependence is when it evolves into flat out managing and controlling behaviour.

In the words of author and codependence expert, Darlene Lancer[13], "managing and controlling behaviors, which include caretaking and enabling, violate others' boundaries. Managing someone's life shows disrespect. It sends the message that the person is incompetent and needs your help. Underneath are your fear and expectations about that person's life.

Lancer describes the controlling codependent person's reasoning as:

I'm uncomfortable, so you have to change.
What you do might hurt me, so I have to watch and control you. I'm responsible for you and have to make sure you make no mistakes (according to me),

---

[13] Lancer, D. (2015). Codependency for Dummies, 2nd Edition..

*Because you can't take care of yourself
(according to me) without my help.*

Ouch. Sound familiar?

And this is often how advice (either from a codependent person, or *to* a codependent person, or both) turns 'caring' into 'controlling'.

"In reality, you can't know what's best for someone else, given his or her individual background, experiences, and desires", Lancer writes. "Managing can start with little things, like giving advice on your husband's clothes, your teenager's diet, or your friend's romance.

Attempts to change, control, and give unwanted advice are codependent patterns that undermine the others' self-esteem. Perhaps you lend a sympathetic ear to their problems and suggest solutions.

Soon, you end up in the role of fixer, counsellor, or cheerleader and become increasingly entangled in their choices and upset that their behavior doesn't meet your expectations.

You begin to watch their every move to see if they're doing the 'right' thing."

When I was first introduced to the concept of codependence and subsequently realised "holy shit that's me", I was initially confused about the difference between being codependent and just being a nice, helpful human being. I couldn't really distinguish between 'caring' and 'codependence'.

A caring person asks about other people's lives, tries to help, offers advice, wants someone to be better. Right?

Well, yes that is right, but I eventually realised there is one huge and glaring and obvious difference between caring and codependence, and that is boundaries.

Caring has, and respects, boundaries.

Caretaking and codependence have no idea what that means.

The psychotherapist, Sharon Martin[14], makes the distinction beautifully.

"Codependents gravitate towards people they can take care of – this could be someone who struggles with addiction, mental or physical illness, emotional immaturity, and so forth", Martin writes.

"As codependents, caretaking feeds our self-esteem, our need to be needed, and gives us a sense of purpose.

---

[14] https://www.livewellwithsharonmartin.com/

We may also hold a false belief that as long as we're needed, we won't be abandoned or rejected. So, caretaking gives us a sense of security."

And then boundaries – or more specifically the lack of boundaries – smashes that sense of security.

Martin again: "Boundaries help to differentiate one person from another. When you have strong boundaries, you're clear about what's your responsibility and what's not. You're aware of your feelings and don't let other people's feelings become your own. You're clear about what you like and dislike. And you understand what you need, and do things to meet those needs."

You just know there's a big but coming ...

"But, codependent caretaking is based on enmeshed boundaries. Codependents try to solve other people's problems or do things for them (which can lead to enabling).

We offer unsolicited advice. We force our ideas and solutions without taking into account what our loved ones want. In other words, our caretaking doesn't always respect their preferences, abilities, and right to self-determination.

In fact, to others, it can feel more like meddling than caring."

But when our codependence is running the show, it messes with our self-awareness so much that we don't feel like we are meddling (if we are the ones giving the unsolicited advice), just as much as we don't think we can make a decision on our own without someone giving us advice (for those constantly getting unsolicited advice). Oh, and before you start freaking out about being codependent and how you must be the only person who feels this way, it's worth noting that a 1999 study[15] estimated that at least 50% and maybe even up to 90% of the population displayed codependent characteristics.

For people who have survived either a childhood trauma or had parents that were either neglectful or enmeshing, that number is even higher.

Codependence is less of a human disorder and more of just ... being human.

———————————————— · ————————————————

[15] Crester, G. & Lombardo, W. (1999). Examining codependency in a college population. College Student Journal, 33(4), 629-637.

Validation.

You know that friend who just keeps asking different people for advice until they find the opinion that matches theirs, and they get the answer they want?

Yep, that.

Be honest. What percentage of the times when you have asked someone for advice, have you already had the answer in mind? Either the answer of what you want them to say, or the answer which you *know* they are going to say?

As any criminal barrister will tell you: never ask a question you don't know the answer to.

In putting this book together, I conducted quite a few studies to get some data about the ways in which we give, get, and use advice.

One of the surveys asked the question: "Do you ever ask for advice, but if that advice doesn't match your own opinion, you go on to ask someone else?

Of the 2,466 people who responded, 1,860 of them (75%) said yes.

Three-quarters of us don't want advice, we want validation. Tell us what we want to hear, not what you think.

If nothing else shows the futility and flat-out silliness of advice, it's got to be that.

But this is nothing new. We have been seeking out people and opinions to validate our own opinions and beliefs, regardless of how silly they are, for generations.

We need to believe in ourselves. And to do that, we need to find people that will tell us what we believe in ourselves is accurate and real. Even if we have to work through a few people to find the ones that will.

But we will find them. And we will believe it.

One of the reasons why tarot readings, astrology, and clairvoyance exists is because people are so desperate to attribute very vague and broad statements to their own personality and their own future.

One of the problems with this readiness to believe in stuff that can't be explained, is that it also displays a propensity to only see things from your own angle.

A big study from 2016[16] tested people who identified as either paranormal psychic believers or sceptics, all of whom had similar levels of education and academic performance, and found that the 'believers' displayed less analytical thinking.

---

[16] Gray, S. J., & Gallo, D. A. (2016). Paranormal psychic believers and skeptics: a large-scale test of the cognitive differences hypothesis. Memory and Cognition, 44, 242-261.

They were more likely to see the world and different situations *only* from their own perspective, and without consideration of others, or the wider community.

And yet, the believers still far outweigh the sceptics.

A Gallup poll conducted in 2005[17], showed that as many as three out of four Americans believed paranormal phenomena was real, and that that belief hadn't really changed since previous polls asked the same question. 42% of people believe in E.S.P., 31% think telepathy is real, and 26% believe in clairvoyance.

When I was researching this book, one of the surveys that I had people complete was about clairvoyance or 'fortune telling'. The 1143 respondents were from all different countries, levels of education, and socio-economic backgrounds.

I got similar results to the Gallup poll, with 27.2% (311 out of 1143) of those polled saying that they 'absolutely believed' in clairvoyance, that people had psychic abilities and could see the future, and what they tell people is real, and should be listened to.

But here's the crazy part. 11.8% (135 out of 1143) of those polled said that they did not believe in clairvoyance or that fortune tellers had some sort of

[17] Gallup. (2005). Three in four Americans believe in paranormal: Little change from similar results in 2001. Retrieved from www.gallup.com/poll/16915/Three-Four-Americans-Believe-Paranormal.aspx

psychic ability, but they 'would still take the advice of the fortune teller and change their life accordingly'.

Seriously.

It's got nothing to do with intelligence, or even how gullible or suggestible someone is. It's more complex than that. Psychology even has a name for it: the Barnum Effect.

Named after the circus and showman, P. T. Barnum who, from all accounts, was not as kind and loving as Hugh Jackman would have us believe.

He is also the person that the phrase 'there is a sucker born every minute' is attributed to (Barnum not Jackman).

The effect is when people positively acknowledge character or personality descriptions that they think are either really accurate of them, or that they would really like to be accurate of them.

My star sign, if you believe in that kind of thing, is Aries. The day I wrote this paragraph, I checked out my 'stars' in the newspaper (is there a more 1983 phrase than that?) and this[18] is what it said:

---

[18] https://www.dailytelegraph.com.au/lifestyle/horoscopes

It's not easy to move a mountain. Success depends on whether the mountain's prepared to move and how much explosive you can access.

OK, well, I can't argue with any of that so far.

Some people make a living out of this kind of work…

Now here I presume that they are talking about the complex work of mountain exploding and not astrology.

Although, it could be some sort of 'in plain sight' double meaning.

and know exactly how much dynamite's needed to create the right kind of result. The question today is how much you know about achieving the seemingly impossible.

OK, using the phrase 'seemingly impossible' is starting to seem like a cry for help or some kind of admission from this astrologer.

> Since you're an adventurous Aries, you have more
> experience than you think.

This is what's known as a 'Barnum statement'.

By reminding you that you are an Aries (whatever that's supposed to mean), and by virtue of that, you are also adventurous, the effect encourages the reader to attribute that desirable personality trait to themselves.

By further reminding you that you 'have more experience than you think' also comforts the reader into thinking that their experience obviously makes this nonsense a whole lot more legitimate and 'sciencey'.

> As long as you approach your mountain
> from the right direction, you really can move it.

So, you know, if you are wondering how to live your life today to reach wealth and success and happiness, I doubt you need much more direction than that right?

The art of this is its reliance on the Barnum Effect. That a bunch of random and really vague sentences will be grasped by someone who is looking for some validation and somehow, it will make sense.

Vagueness is the key, as witnessed by the same horoscope for today, but this time for people who identify as Geminis.

Is it easy to see straight ahead? An ophthalmologist might give you one answer, a psychoanalyst another. There are lots of different factors that affect our ability to perceive accurately what's right in front of our noses. But none of them are as brilliant at deceiving us as our imagination. When we're overly optimistic, or pessimistic, it affects our judgement. And our vision gets hazy. As Mercury prepares to turn retrograde, you're able to recognise something you've been looking at. Yet, until now, have been unable to identify fully.

I mean, it's genius really.

89 words that together mean absolutely nothing and yet someone – presumably only those who are born between May 22 and June 22 – will understand fully, be

totally able to attach them to something they've 'been looking at', and feel validated.

And before you get too high and mighty and say 'well, I don't believe in that garbage', remember around 1 in 8 of people that I polled don't believe it either, but would 'change their life' according to what is said to them by someone who has 'the gift'.

Luckily though, science – as usual – comes to the rescue.

A scientist named Bertram Forer was interested in this effect, and decided to see if he could test out its validity scientifically.

He conducted 'personality testing' on a bunch of psychology students and when he gave them their personalised results from the testing, he asked them how accurate the results were.

Some of the vague descriptions included in the results were statements like:

You have a great deal of unused capacity, which you have not turned to your advantage.

You have a tendency to be critical of yourself.

You have a great need for other people to like and admire you.

And one which I can only assume made the nerdy scientist chuckle to himself for including:

You pride yourself as an independent thinker and do not accept other statements without satisfactory proof.

So, the respondents all get their personality test results back, and Forer asks them how accurate they were. Amazingly, the overwhelming majority of the students said that the descriptions were either absolutely or very close to being correct about them.

The catch?

Every student was given exactly the same personality test result, regardless of how they answered the testing questions.

Ladies and gentlemen: the Barnum Effect.

And this is also the problem with advice that is sought by people to achieve some kind of validation of an idea or opinion that they already hold.

We will find what we are looking for, if we look for it hard enough.

As you might know, I worked at Facebook for a few years when it was first growing into the phenomenon it is today.

I knew, and was privy to, a lot of things that other people didn't know about how that business ran, how the products worked, and what compelled people to feel 'addicted' to social media.

While I was working there, and sadly still, there was a rumour that Facebook was listening to conversations and private interactions of users via their mobile phones.

Once Facebook had eavesdropped on your conversation and knew what you were interested in or talking about, the rumour goes that you then get delivered an ad for that very thing in your news feed.

When I would speak at a conference or event when I worked there, it was the one question that I could always guarantee being asked of me when I was on stage during a Q&A.

If someone believed that it was true, there was almost no way that I could convince them otherwise, and that includes my closest friends and family.

Most of my clients and audiences when I was working there were small business owners who advertised regularly on the platform, often spending a lot of their marketing and advertising budget to do so.

I would ask these users, if Facebook was listening to people's conversations, and then serving ads to them based on those conversations, why weren't they, as advertisers, able to put some of their spend into that ad product?

I mean, if it were true, it would pretty much be the only ad spend I would be investing.

But despite me denying the rumour at least ten times a week on stage, and in the media, and the CEO testifying before the US Congress that it wasn't happening, the rumour continued, and continues today.

"OK, but I was talking about lawn fertiliser to my mate and then all of a sudden I got an ad for lawn fertiliser."

"Yeah Nick, I hear what you're saying, but my sister and her husband were in their kitchen talking about worming tablets for their chihuahua, and then she got an ad for worming tablets – specifically for chihuahuas!"

"Well explain this one then. I was talking to my husband about a new plastic bin for our laundry, but how I only wanted one if it was purple. Then, wouldn't you know it, I get an ad for laundry bins, but the one pictured in the ad is purple!"

So, what's the explanation for all that?

Well, there are two things going on. One: the huge amount of data that you have freely given to social media platforms about yourself, your community, your friends and family, your likes and dislikes, how you shop, what you buy, and why you buy it.

And two: something called the Baader-Meinhof Phenomenon. Also called 'frequency illusion', Baader-Meinhof is a form of cognitive bias that makes us more aware of seeing, hearing, and feeling certain things after we have been given a stimulus related to that thing.

The increase in awareness of something, creates an illusion of that thing being regularly around us all of a sudden.

When you buy a red Mazda hatchback, all of a sudden you start seeing other red Mazda hatchbacks everywhere.

Or you learn a new word that you have never even heard before, and then in the following week you see and hear that word being used all over the place.

There aren't more red hatchbacks around now, something called 'selective attention' is just making you more and more aware of them compared to other cars.

And it's not that everyone else has suddenly learned and is using *your* new word this week, they have always been using it. You just didn't know what the word was or what it meant before this week.

So no, although some people really want (and some seem to actually *need*) the listening phone thing to be real, it's not. Lots and lots of people will tell you it's true, and if you already think it's true, you're only likely to listen to those people anyway.

I was recently watching the comedian Amy Schumer's Netflix special and she was talking about drinking while she was pregnant. She told the story of asking her most responsible friend, a nurse, what her opinion was on pregnant women having a drink.

This responsible friend suggested that she should probably just skip it and not have anything to drink before the baby was born. Schumer responded "yeah OK, that makes sense", but then went an asked a slightly more 'lenient' friend what her thoughts on drinking when pregnant were.

"A glass a week is probably fine", the friend responded and Schumer was much more encouraged and felt better about her answer than the one her more responsible friend had given her.

To paraphrase, Schumer continues through to, in her words, her "most dirtbag, deadbeat friend" to get the advice that she actually wanted to hear, and to validate that she could drink whatever she wanted in whatever quantities.

It was for comedic effect, she said she didn't drink a drop while she was pregnant, but it illustrates what a lot of us do every day: keep asking until you find the answer you want.

If there's anything that shows the futility and silliness of advice (both giving and getting) it's that. We only ask the questions we know the answer of already, and we seek out the people who are most likely to validate our beliefs, to ask those questions of.

It's easy to tell the people who are asking your advice just to validate their own already-held belief though: their reaction to your answer.

In an instant of you giving your advice they are either smugly pleased and visibly reassured that what they were thinking was right *and* that they picked the right person to validate them, or they look shocked, surprised, or even a bit pissed off with your answer that doesn't match their pre-determined one.

One reason for the asking-advice-for-validation thing being so prevalent, is that humans are basically hopeless at receiving compliments.

And because we suck at that, we seek out other less-obvious ways to get support and reassurance.

So often when we are confronted (I used that word purposely because for many people being complimented is something close to being attacked for some reason) with someone saying something nice to us or about us, we immediately fend it away rather than accepting it.

"Hey, I like your hair that way."

"Really? I don't know,
it's shorter than I usually have it."

"That's a nice dress."

"This old rag? I bought it ages ago,
it doesn't really fit me anymore either."

"You're a great parent."

"Pffft, no way.
YOU are the great parent, not me."

And finally, one for all of the codependents:

"You did a really good job on that."

"No, I couldn't have done it without you."

Argghh, seriously.

You know what happens when someone says something nice to you and you deny it, and deflect it, and basically tell them they are wrong?

They store that reaction away in the crappy part of their brain that tells them not to do that again.

With you or anyone else.

Don't take a chance again to be kind out loud because you will get rejected.

Don't trust your thoughts and feelings because obviously you're an idiot who doesn't know what looks good and what doesn't.

It's the kind of interaction we never give a second thought to. But *they* do.

In recent years, I have gotten a lot better at receiving a compliment by using a little hack that my own therapist gave me a little while ago.

His tip? Gratitude with brevity.

Even though my brain still works the same way as others when it first hears something nice being said to me by someone else: deflect, deny, downplay, discount, I have actually learnt to listen to the compliment, hear what they have said, and the spirit in which it was said, and then just say "thanks".

That's it.

OK, it's not that great a hack, but it works really well.

It stops me from waffling on about how wrong they are to give me a compliment in the first place, and it makes the other person feel heard and recognised. They are grateful for your gratitude.

And I know this, because I know what the face of someone looks like who has just been thanked for their compliment.

And it's the face of someone who likes how they are feeling in that moment, and are much more likely to deliver another compliment to me – or importantly, someone else – in the future too.

But here's the other thing about asking for validation through advice.

Let's use the analogy of the clothes you are going to wear to a party. You ask your partner or your friend or your roommate if they think it looks OK, and they give you an opinion that usually only has two options: "it looks good", or ... "I dunno, maybe?"

But the thing is: *you bought the clothes*.

You thought they suited your style and looked good on you.

You made an adult decision and backed yourself that you were right.

And now you are willing to throw all of that away on the opinion of another person who wasn't even involved in the buying decision, probably doesn't have the same sense of style you have, and certainly doesn't know how you feel when you are wearing those clothes!

It's a weird thing to do.

What difference does it make if you are the only person who likes those clothes?

They're *your* clothes, and *you like them*!

————————————— · —————————————

To have someone to blame.

You know what makes the pain and embarrassment of making a mistake hurt just a bit less? Having someone else to blame for it.

And being able to shift responsibility for something going badly is, for some people, the sole reason you will be asked for advice in the first place.

And it's not just small or trivial things that some of these people want to entangle you in.

I have been asked my opinion on whether someone should take a job in a completely different industry (and country).

A friend has asked me whether she should keep a baby she was pregnant with.

Too many people have weirdly asked *me* if they should stay in their marriage or relationship.

And I've even been asked for my advice on whether someone should go through with their wedding *while* we were standing in the church immediately before their wedding.

"I knew I should never have had this baby. You were the one who told me it would be OK."

"I've only had the job for two months and I'm miserable and I don't know what I'm doing."

"My spouse is a douche. I should never have listened to you that day."

I don't know, perhaps four minutes before your bride walked down the aisle to marry you wasn't the ideal time to ask my opinion?

Some people get very conditioned to be in a blame and drama trap, and they are not even aware they are doing it – and involving you.

American Psychiatrist, Dr. Stephen B. Karpman[19] did a lot of work on this blame and problem solver game that he eloquently described as the Karpman Drama Triangle. He described three roles, the victim, the rescuer, and the persecutor, and called them the three faces of drama.

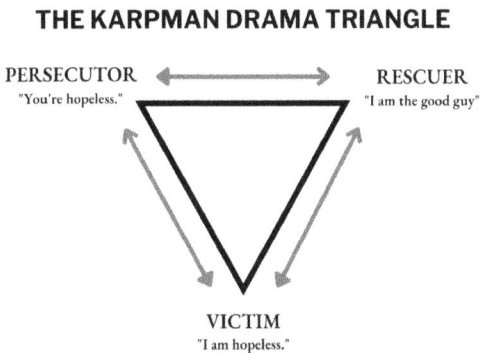

THE KARPMAN DRAMA TRIANGLE

PERSECUTOR
"You're hopeless."

RESCUER
"I am the good guy"

VICTIM
"I am hopeless."

---

[19] https://karpmandramatriangle.com/

The Persecutor attacks the victim:

"You're hopeless.
You can't do anything right.
You're to blame."

The Victim replies helplessly:

"I am hopeless.
I can't do anything right.
But it's not my fault."

The Rescuer steps in:

"I am the good guy.
Come here, I can help you.
I don't care if it's your fault,
I will make everything OK."

The drama only comes when there is a switching of roles.

The Victim eventually gets sick of everyone piling on them and having to put up with their crap, and lashes out (becomes the persecutor).

Then they realise that they were harsh in her lashing out and tries to repair the situation (becoming the rescuer).

Some people can fill, not just one, but all of the roles over time in a relationship.

Some even manage it in the space of a conversation.

Mary (Victim):

"God, I hate my sister, she has done it again."

John (Rescuer):

"Oh no, what happened?"

Mary (Victim):

"Like I told you last time, she has gone right off at me for something I didn't even do."

John (Rescuer):

"Did you speak to your mum about it?"

Mary (now the Persecutor):

"Are you serious? You know that would just make things a million times worse. You never listen to me!"

John (now the Victim):

"Hey! I was just trying to help you.
Don't include me in your family's shit
if you don't want my opinion or my help."

Mary (now the Victim):

"You're right.
I'm sorry.
I didn't mean to yell.
Can I get you a coffee or something?"

John (now the Persecutor):

"No. Just leave me alone.
I'm sick of your shit.
I don't need you."

Be honest with yourself, what's your normal role?

I use this in my therapy a lot. And it's almost never that someone is stuck in the same role consistently. Mind you, being in the same one of these three pretty crappy roles forever doesn't sound that great either.

A consistent theme with my clients in regards to the triangle is this: client is in a difficult or dying relationship with their spouse (Victim). Instead of directing their anger and energy towards their partner to try to fix (or leave) the relationship, they instead become really angry at their partner's family and friends, and ex-partners and the world in general (Persecutor).

Meanwhile, they have their kids in the triangle with them too, and they dote and enmesh their children telling them they are not part of the relationship difficulty, but secretly hoping to win them on to their side for after the inevitable break up (Rescuer).

That's an extreme example, but I see a version of that dynamic play out in my therapy practice a few times every day.

The blaming bit comes into it because some people seem very comfortable in the triangle and will drag a WMAG into the role of rescuer, only to turn them into the persecutor if it all goes ass-up.

All care, no responsibility.

When we are in the triangle we just go round and round and round, until we can either somehow get into the centre of the triangle, or we can learn to push back on the power of the other people in the triangle.

Ultimately though, once the drama triangle can be seen for what it is, the key to unlocking the game, is to no longer play.

———————————————— · ————————————————

Do they even want your advice?

Maybe they want something else from you?

Aside from someone literally saying to you, "hey can I get your advice?", can you be totally sure your input is even being asked for, far less listened to?

A lot of people struggle to just listen to someone expressing a problem or talking about a difficult situation in their life, and not jump in straight away with a solution.

Men, I'm looking at you.

Could it be possible that every single time a friend told you something that was going on for them, what they wanted was for you to give them advice, and that the advice you gave then solved what was going on for them?

Spoiler alert: no, it can't be.

Notice that I didn't just say 'every single time a friend has a problem' and that 'that advice solved their problem'?

That's because it isn't always. Sometimes people just have stuff that they are thinking about, being bothered by, wanting to improve, or even wanting to celebrate the end of.

The trouble with the WMAG's is that they are too busy loading up their advice cannon to see whether it's actually needed.

Honestly, this isn't something I started to get better at until I started working as a therapist. The irony is that in that situation, the majority of my clients would absolutely love me to tell them what to do.

The truth, of course, is that they really need to work that out on their own.

Therapy isn't being taught what to think, it's being helped with *how* to think.

And, for the most part, it's about listening. Without judgement. Without pity. And without shame.

If only all of our interactions with people were like that.

There is an extra difficulty here that a lot of people miss though.

Conventional wisdom would say that if you want someone to just listen to you and not try to fix everything, you should say to them something along the lines of "just listen and don't try to fix everything", right?

I have had that said to me, and at least some of those times I was just listening and I wasn't trying to fix everything.

And, it hurt.

Saying that to another person can make them feel like they are not an equal partner in the friendship.

That they are in an adversarial relationship. That there is a power imbalance between you.

One of you is a problem-holder, the other a problem-solver.

Those roles can feel constant and pre-defined, and that construct can be difficult to negotiate when the problem-solver actually has a problem that they need help with.

It is, however, important to have your needs met.

If someone (in your opinion) never listens and always suggests things that might fix a problem, you may have to mention that what you need is someone to just hear you out right now.

You might also find that some positive reinforcement once they have listened and heard you and not suggested any fixes, will see them adopt that strategy again in the future.

Like a seal at Sea World being thrown a fish after balancing a beach ball on its nose, men - I mean people who don't listen and just try to fix everything - are simple creatures.

CHAPTER 2:

Why do people give advice?

So, what makes us so convinced that we have the answers that somebody else so desperately needs?

What have we learnt over the course of our lives that has lead us to the point where we know what somebody needs to do, and have somehow amassed the incredible arrogance that encourages us to tell them?

Is it in our nature to advise?

Or is it nurture?

Are we so comfortable with having been given advice all of our lives that we just eventually reach an age where we take the reins ourselves and start dishing out advice to anyone who will listen?

It is somehow linked to age. Kids don't give advice, not even really to other kids. They might recite rules that have been told to them by their family or school teachers, but they generally don't give out life advice to other kids.

So what are some of the reasons people give advice, well-meaning or otherwise?

They think they are helping.

A recent conversation with a client went like this:

Client:

"So, I have been talking to
my friend Jenny. She recently left
her husband and so I think I will too."

Me:

"OK, where has this come from?
I thought you were getting along
pretty well now after all the
work you have both done?

Client:

"No, we are. But I just see how happy
and content Jenny is now, and she said she
has never been calmer or more interested
in life and everything it has to offer now.
So I want that too."

Jenny[20], bless her, thought she was helping – either my client or maybe just herself – by telling my client how great her new life was. But there are two significant factors here that could make this exchange very, very unhelpful.

1. My client is making a big permanent decision based on basically the hearsay of her friend, who obviously is not living the same life with the same idiosyncrasies and hopes and struggles as her.

Their husbands are completely different people, and my client and Jenny are completely different people too!

They have different families, different kids, different jobs, different levels of income and financial security, they live in different suburbs, they have been with their husbands for different amounts of time. You can see where I'm going here right? They are different.

2. Jenny might actually be full of it.

Nobody wants to go through a huge relationship and life upheaval, only to realise it was a mistake and they have done the wrong thing and they really miss their own life.

I don't know if that's true for Jenny, but that's the point, only Jenny does.

---

[20] Jenny is such a generic alias. I was going to go with Karen, but God knows they have been through enough. I'm sure one of them has mentioned it to you…

Maybe a more helpful message to come from Jenny – if she needs to send one at all – might be "I am happy, it was the right decision for me, but it might not be for everyone".

Maybe Jenny should be a therapist.

Mostly, WMAG's really do think they are helping.

For whatever drives the WMAG to give someone else the benefit of their wisdom, they are not giving out malicious or harmful advice.

In fact, most of the advice that WMAG are throwing around could actually be helpful. The thing is, they don't know whether the person they are advising is the right person to be getting it, and therefore, they don't know whether the recipient will be helped.

How could they? They just don't know enough about that person or their life or circumstance.

———————————— · ————————————

They think they know better.

I mean, let's face it, there aren't many of us who don't think our long-held and really indoctrinated core beliefs are wrong, right?

Whether they have some relevant life experience to bolster their advice with or not, one of the main reasons that people offer someone else advice is because they just know what's better for someone else than that person obviously does.

They can see it more clearly because they are looking at with objective eyes. But the truth of someone thinking they know better than you – and then offering you advice on the back of that belief – is that you obviously don't know what's good for you, that you don't know yourself as well as they do, and that you are basically a bit of a dill.

Anybody who starts a sentence with "you know what you should do?" is a huge red flag for me.

I mean, I am envious of that kind of self-confidence that would make you think it's OK for you to not only offer advice – probably unsolicited – but to then preface it with basically a command.

That's pretty confident.

There's another consideration here too. What if they *do* know better?

Let's say a friend gives you advice on a situation you are going through that they have recently been through themselves, and they are in pretty much the exact same situation and circumstance as you, and they are pretty much the same person as you.

They consider their advice to you to be both valid and helpful, and you accept their advice because you can accept that, given their recent experience with the same circumstance, they actually might know better than you what to do.

You follow their advice, and the outcome is whatever it is.

But how does that affect you? I mean in the future and ongoing from that.

You have made a decision completely based off someone else's advice (albeit someone with a similar recent experience and so on), but do you now have the outcome that *you* wanted, or the outcome that *they* wanted?

And the next time you have to make a decision, are you more or less likely to back yourself and your own experience and intelligence, or look for someone else to basically make that decision for you again?

If I am going to fuck something up, I want it to be because I thought I wouldn't.

My life has been full of lessons, but the ones that I have learnt the most from have been the ones where I was doing the teaching.

———————————————— . ————————————————

They want to control someone.

There is definitely an element of control in the giving of advice.

It requires an inherent power imbalance: one person either vulnerably asking for advice, or involuntarily receiving unsolicited advice, from someone who is feeling more in control, and wanting to control the other.

The most obvious example of this is the parent-child relationship.

When parents feel like they need to control their child a little more tightly, often it's advice they go to.

When they want their child to go to the university that they want them to.

When they want them to get the job that they think would be perfect for them.

When they want them to marry the girl that they just know is their ideal life partner.

And it works too, because we are so conditioned to take the advice (and/or control and direction) from our parents, that whatever they say invariably seems like the right option to pursue.

But you know what else a controlling person does? They never accept responsibility or blame for anything that you do as a result of their control.

Advice is often delivered in this dynamic with 'all care but no responsibility' attached to it.

_____ . _____

They want to reduce their own anxiety.

For someone (like me) who lives with a generalised anxiety, giving advice can actually be therapeutic.

Nothing takes the focus of your own shit more than focussing on someone else's.

Also, telling someone else what they should do in order to sort their stuff out and bring some order and control to their lives, takes a big step towards the advice-giver feeling an increased level of control over their own chaotic lives.

_____ . _____

They want to show how smart they are.

Do you think anyone gives advice to someone who they believe is smarter or wiser than them?

Does anyone without a degree in astrophysics give astrophysics advice to a professor of astrophysics?[21]

Whether they mean to or not, people give advice to other people who they hold in less esteem than themselves.

People give advice to people they think are dumber than them, and that's why they haven't worked out the solution without their advice already.

---

[21] Well, actually, prior to 2020, I would have always said the answer to this question was no, but these days I'm not so sure.

They are Spelling Correctors.

You know who are the ultimate givers of advice that nobody asked for? Spelling Correctors.

Those special people who just can't help themselves but correct someone else (even people they don't know) when they type *your* instead of *you're*, or *there* instead of *their*.

Even science agrees that these people are ... well, jerks.

In 2016, researchers from the University of Michigan examined the motivations behind people who corrected other people's spelling and grammar, and their study[22] found that these people mostly have "less agreeable personalities".

Someone with a 'less agreeable personality' is science researcher code for 'dicks'.

I mean think about it: what does a Spelling Corrector get out of it when they point out that someone else doesn't know how to spell something correctly, or how to use the proper grammar in a sentence?

[22] Boland, J. & Queen, R. (2016). If You're House Is Still Available, Send Me an Email: Personality Influences Reactions to Written Errors in Email Messages. PloS One, 11(3), e0149885-e01498885

The only thing it can give the Spelling Corrector is a sense of superiority.

That they know something someone else doesn't.

That they are smarter than someone else.

And, worse still, they want to rub the other person's nose in it.

I reckon these people are, more often than not, also people who have very little power or agency over their own life.

They are small, and mean. But boy, can they spell.

———————————— . ————————————

They have no power elsewhere in their life.

And speaking of people who have no power in their life...

Another big reason why people dish out advice is to prove to themselves, and to anyone else who cares, that they still have a bit of authority to throw around the place.

Even when they have no tangible life experience to back up their advice and opinions.

Someone that I have known most of my life is currently in a pretty miserable, sad, and powerless relationship with someone who controls most of her decisions, her spending, and her happiness.

That doesn't stop her from dishing out opinions about life and relationships, including telling other women (and men) that they should "escape" their current relationship with the controlling monster they are with.

I have heard her give this advice with my own ears.

The pursuit of feeling power is a massive contributor to people giving advice to others.

Associate Professor of Psychology at Singapore Management University, Michael Schaerer[23], and his

---

[23] @michaelschaerer

colleagues ran a series of studies in 2018 to see what influence advice-giving had on a person's feeling of power.

In the first study, participants were asked to imagine a situation in which they gave someone advice as part of an everyday conversation.

They were then asked to give a measurement of how much power they felt when they did that, and everyone who had given advice said that they were feeling more powerful now.

OK, simple enough.

The second and third study they ran then looked at whether people gave advice in order to feel more powerful.

Again, the people who wanted to feel more power were also more likely to be the ones giving out advice.

The final study looked into the practice of giving out advice on an online platform. The participants were split into two groups: those that were told that the person they gave the advice to read it, or they didn't bother reading the advice they gave.

Interestingly, this still showed that if people wanted to feel more powerful, giving advice would help them feel that way, but just as interestingly, when they were told that their advice had either been ignored or not read at all, they felt *less* powerful.

These studies showed that, even if the pursuit of power wasn't a motivating factor for people, when they gave advice to someone, they still felt more powerful.

However, it also showed that the real power was not in giving advice, it was in that advice being received, and someone else being interested in it.

Humans are funny.

———————————————— · ————————————————

They can't see past their own rigidity.

The advice-giving personality tends to be a fairly rigid one.

Their propensity for black and white thinking not only ensures they have a plan and advice ready to go at any time for anyone who asks, but it also convinces them that their solution is the only possible one.

This 'if this, then that' way of thinking empowers them with knowledge that they think is not only legitimate and true, but also something that needs to be shared with everyone, whether they ask for it or not.

There's no grey. Something just is, or it isn't.

And so much of that thinking has been transplanted into them by their parents, who got it from their parents, and so on.

It's rarely new or modern thinking, it's mostly nostalgic thinking, and the longer it has been held within a family line, the more black and white it becomes.

I remember listening to a couple who are friends of mine, talking to their teenage son who was in high school, but wanted to drop out to start a trade in carpentry.

The son was explaining to them that he had already sourced and committed to a full-time job, and a four-year apprenticeship linked to that job, and that it was something that he really wanted to do and was actually pretty excited about doing it.

"No, you have to finish high school", his mum responded.

"You can't go to uni if you don't finish high school", said his dad.

"But I don't want to go to uni, and I don't want to finish high school", their son explained pretty reasonably.

But there was no changing his parents' black and white thinking about this.

They had both been told that they had to finish school, and they had to go to university, and come hell or high water, their children were going to do the same.

The son ended up staying at high school, and every time I asked him how he was going through that time, he just seemed more and more unhappy and stunted.

And then, finally, after three more years of battling through high school he graduated and ... he is now an apprentice carpenter.

And happy.

They have to be right.

This one stings because, for a long time, I was definitely this guy.

Not only did I need to *feel* right, but for some reason I really needed you to know I *was* right.

But then, eventually, I realised that the only way to learn and grow is to – at least some of the time – accept that I didn't know everything already.

Also, those people (like I used to be) who have to argue and debate over every tiny little detail that they are sure they are right about and that probably doesn't matter anyway?

Yep, those people are dicks.

I don't want to be that guy any more.

Those people though, the ones that have to be right all the time, they are also huge advice givers.

I mean, it's very difficult for them to stop short at just telling you why you are wrong, without then expanding on what you should do, or think, or feel, to be right.

Arrghh, I really don't like that part of me.

They think it's impressive.

We mostly want to impress other people.

It's kind of how we have always been rewarded. Impress the teacher, you get better marks. Impress the girl, you get to take her to the movies. Impress her enough, she might marry you. Impress your boss, you might get a raise.

And so on.

But as the author Mark Manson writes, it's fraught with danger. "The reason trying to impress people rarely works out very well, is because human beings are wired to not simply look at surface-level behaviors when judging another person's character, but to also look at their intentions and motivations for each behavior.

So, you can do a cool action, but if you're doing it because you're insecure and want people to like you, people will see through it and find you annoying."

I'm pretty sure we all know that guy in our life. Hot tip: if you don't know that person, you probably *are* that person.

"This is why one-uppers", Manson writes, "people who take what you say and then tell you how they've done something bigger or better than that – are so annoying.

They're trying to impress us, to dominate us, to show superiority over us. And the fact that they're trying to be superior proves to us that they're not."

───────────────── . ─────────────────

They are suckers for nostalgia.

Advice is steeped in that kind of nostalgia.

"My grandfather told my Dad this bit of advice, and now I'm going to give it to you" kind of thing.

But nostalgia can be helpful as a tool for emotional regulation, and even as a coping strategy for loneliness[24].

I think moreover, it is a negative thing that keeps us trapped in somebody else's past, and dishing out archaic and outdated advice from there.

Psychologist and trauma expert, Dr. Valentina Stoycheva writes that the difference between nostalgia being helpful or harmful is the difference between "incorporating the positive emotions of reminiscing into the present versus renouncing the present for the sake of reinstating and perpetually reliving some moment in the past."

She believes that some people over-indulge with nostalgia which causes them to never be happy with the present, because they are glorifying some moment from their past.

Dr. Stoycheva also warns that this holding on to nostalgia can be harmful, both at a personal level (for instance, a person using cosmetic surgery in an

[24] Wildschut, T., Sedikides, C., Arndt, J. & Routledge, C. (2006). Nostalgia: Content, triggers, functions. Journal of Personality and Social Psychology, 91(5), 975-993.

unhealthy way to keep themselves looking the way they used to), and at a societal level (for example, wishing for the good old days but casually ignoring the fact that the 'good old days' were also when not everyone could vote, or there was segregation, or homophobia, or ignored family violence and trauma, and so on.

And a lot of advice coming from these nostalgia lovers is also coming from the good old days.

Worth noting.

_____ · _____

They literally can't help themselves.

Advice-givers are governed a lot more by their compulsion to give advice than their self-awareness of whether their advice is helpful, or has even been asked for.

Therefore, the drive to share their advice doesn't come from a mindful or thoughtful place, it's more of a compulsion, something they can't immediately control.

And that compulsion is fed by the rest of us rarely pushing back on that advice.

When the person who is addicted to giving advice is never pulled up on it, or called out for it, they continue to do it. Why wouldn't they?

The key for these people to reduce their indiscriminate-machine-gun-advice-giving is self-awareness. But while ever the rest of us give them allowances, and say things like "it's just her way", the longer their path to self-awareness will be.

—————————————— · ——————————————

They need to consolidate their 'better-than' (and your 'less-than') position.

Often, the actual advice people are giving someone else is more symptomatic of their relationship with them than a necessary exchange of information or knowledge.

Yes, they are offering you a solution to the problem you have asked them about (if you *have* even asked them about it), but what they are actually doing is reminding you that you are less than them. That your life experience is them than them. That your intelligence and street-smarts are less than them. That you need them in order to be functional in your own life.

It's not always a malicious and conscious thing.

Sometimes, it's more of that nostalgic crap creeping in again.

You have always been the less-informed, younger, dumber one, and that's an arrangement they feel comfortable with, so they will do whatever they can to preserve it as long as they can.

Sometimes, as mentioned above, they are too rigid in their thinking to change, or they have no power in their life other than over you, or they just can't seem to help themselves.

But for someone to hold a space over us where they feel superior, or better-than, and by virtue of that we feel less-than or inadequate or unimportant, we first have to give them that space, and then keep providing them that space from then on.

Science agrees.

A 2018 study[25] found that people wanted to give advice only to those who they felt they have a power imbalance over.

They found that giving advice makes the advice-giver believe that the 'lesser' person was not only able to influenced, but also that they *needed* their help.

The researchers concluded that giving advice was a 'subtle route to a sense of power'.

If we really believe that they are not better than us – that nobody is better than us – then we can take back that space, and in doing so take back some of our power.

And the first step for that is to stop asking for, and stop listening to, advice from them.

[25] Schaerer, Tost, L. P., Huang, L., Gino, F., & Larrick, R. (2018). Advice Giving: A Subtle Pathway to Power. Personality & Social Psychology Bulletin, 44(5), 746–761.

They do it for themselves.

Studies have also shown that there is definitely something in it for the advice-givers, whether it's an increased sense of their own power, an increase in their self-esteem, a sense of validation that they are right (again), or even better marks at school and university!

A 2019[26] study found that people who dish out advice – even if that advice wasn't asked for – do better academically.

However, the same study also suggested that this was at the potential detriment of those that they were giving advice to.

---

[26] Eskreis-Winkier, Milkman, K. L., Gromet, D. M., & Duckworth, A. L. (2019). A large-scale field experiment shows giving advice improves academic outcomes for the advisor. Proceedings of the National Academy of Sciences - PNAS, 116(30), 14808–14810.

To profit from good advice requires more wisdom than to give it.

Wilson Mizner

CHAPTER 3:

Why giving advice is
a terrible idea.

There are hundreds of reasons why giving advice is a bad idea. I've narrowed them down to a few big ones.

The arguments against giving advice range from you not having the same experience or situation to the person you are advising, you inserting yourself into something you might not really want to be part of, or responsible for if it goes badly, right through to whether you were even asked for your advice or not.

There are so many reasons why I think giving advice is a terrible idea. Here's a few.

You don't know the whole story.

You can't possibly know.

At best you only know one side of the story (the side that you have been told), if you've even been told the whole of that.

Not to mention that their side of the story is dripping in their own biases and misunderstandings too.

What a mess.

I find that people possess something of a playbook of advice for every situation, regardless of the individuality or nuance of each one.

For instance, if someone tells them they have been cheated on, their advice is always "you have to leave them".

When someone tells them they were overlooked for a promotion at work for the third time, their advice is always "you should quit that job".

When someone tells them their adult son is moving back home but paying no rent other than just helping out around the house a bit, their response is always "well he should be paying rent and don't be a pushover."

The advice-giver doesn't know the intricacies of their relationship or what has happened before. They don't know that they are actually really poor at their job and the others chosen for the promotions were much better qualified. And they don't know that the adult son is moving home to care for them because they are in the initial stages of dementia and really need their help.

Even if someone tells you 'the full story', there is still undoubtedly other parts, other players, and other reasons why, that you are not being told.

———————————————— · ————————————————

You are in the way of growth.

Something that therapists and social scientists talk about a lot is a person's capacity.

What they mean is basically what would be the person's potential if they were left to develop it fully by themselves? What can they handle? And where they are not living up to it right now?

A big part of a person's capacity is their ability to make decisions for themselves, to self-actualise as Maslow put it, and whether they were able to get there autonomously or not.

If you are constantly telling someone what to do, and what not to do, where is the autonomous growth going to come from?

Aren't they just going to end up being a (probably poor) duplicate of you?

I hear a lot people saying that they give advice to someone because they don't want them to make the same mistakes as they did.

But who's to say they will?

And further, who's to say that *their* outcome will be a mistake as it was in *your* life?

I once had an opportunity to exit and sell one of the few startup businesses I started that was actually successful and profitable, and get a corporate job.

Quite a few people told me it was a bad idea and that I should keep growing the business, but I knew inside me that I needed what this new job could offer me in order to grow and achieve more in my life in the future.

I backed myself and I was right.

Those people giving me the advice to stay where I was would have, for their own reasons, negatively affected my growth by limiting my capacity to grow.

If someone is to flourish and thrive, or struggle and stagnate, it needs to be in line with their own capacity, not yours.

———————————————— · ————————————————

You don't know what you don't know.

But that's unlikely to stop you.

Often, the loudest – and quickest – person to pipe up when they think you need some help is the very same person who is the least equipped to help you.

It even has a name: The Dunning-Kruger effect.

It is a cognitive bias where someone over-estimates their level of understanding and competence in a certain area. I know a few people who suffer with it (or at least they make other people suffer with it).

The old Dunning-Kruger is a double-edged sword too.

While the people who know nothing about the subject over-estimate their level of knowledge, those who know more about a topic also under-estimate themselves because they are also more aware of the gaps in their knowledge.

In terms of advice, this means that the first people to contribute their advice, are also most likely to be the people who know nothing.

On the back of a global pandemic, during which all sorts of different people professed to be experts in epidemiology and disease control, this has never been more evident.

One of my therapy clients has depression and, at times, quite profound anxiety.

She takes medication for her mood disorder, and has been doing a lot of work on her marriage, as has her partner with his own therapist. She has been doing really well, and so a recent conversation I had with her was a bit jarring.

"Nigel[27] (her husband) has Narcissistic Personality Disorder" she told me. "That's why he is how he is and why our relationship has been so difficult".

I have never actually met Nigel as I only work with her.

"Oh, does he?", I asked. "It's actually much rarer than people think with only three or four per cent of people having it so that's interesting. Did a psychiatrist or psychologist diagnose him?"

"No, Karen did. She said he is a lot like her sister's husband and he is a narcissist. She also told me that I don't really have depression I'm just in a crappy marriage, and that I should finally leave him, and stop taking my anti-depressant, and only use aromatherapy and exercise from now on."

---

[27] Not his real name. If your name is Nigel and you are a Narcissist, this story really isn't about you. Not everything is about you OK?

"Oh, is Karen a mental health professional?", I ask.

"Sort of, she's my hairdresser."

Honestly, I wish this was the only time I have ever had a conversation that is frighteningly similar to that one.

Fortunately, the Dunning-Kruger mob are easier to spot than you think. They actually out themselves, you just have to listen to what they say. They often start a sentence with, "Look, I'm not a climate scientist or anything, but ..."

———————————— · ————————————

You have a different experience to them.

It's not always just a case of substituting yourself into or out of a situation, and being able to give the best advice to someone based on what your experience has been in the past.

The person who advises the other person that's been cheated on to leave their partner, might be coming from the angle of their experience where they didn't leave the partner and got cheated on again.

That doesn't mean that's going to happen this time.

You might have had a bad experience starting your own business which then failed and you lost a stack of money, but that doesn't mean the person you are advising not to start *their* own business is going to have the same fate.

None of our experiences in life are the same really.

They might be similar, but humans are much too individual and full of nuance to lob us all in together and expect the same outcome from every situation.

To assume you know the exact effect something is going to have on someone else's life – far less that you are taking into account all of their life experience and vagaries to this point – is naïve at best, and arrogant at worst.

But that's what we do when we give advice based on our own life experience.

We are saying, 'hey, this is what I learned when it happened to me, and therefore you can assume that it's going to occur in exactly the same way for you'.

_____ · _____

You are not supporting them, you are judging them.

It's very difficult to give someone advice without first judging them in some way, and usually that judgement ending with you feeling superior in some way.

When someone gives you advice – whether it's been asked for or not – this might be actually what they are saying from a place of judgement:

You are not smart enough to
work this out for yourself.

You have made some terrible decisions
in the past, so I can't imagine you are
going to make a good decision here
without my help.

I don't trust you.

You are unable to do this without me.

It's hard to disconnect the judgement from advice-giving. After all, if someone has asked you what they should do with their life, they are opening themselves up to be judged in this way.

Maybe they are saying to themselves:

I am not smart enough to
work this out for myself.

I have made some terrible decisions
in the past, so I can't imagine I am
going to make a good decision here
without your help.

I don't trust myself and my
own judgement.

I am unable to do this without you.

You are probably just telling them what they want to hear.

This is one of the great disappointments for a lot of people when they first engaged with therapy.

They really want an answer.

They really want to be told what to do and how to fix something.

And they *really* want it to match what they already had in mind.

That's not the job of therapy though, of course. It's not about being given answers, it's about *finding* answers.

The fact that even the most distressed and distracted people still have quite a clear picture in their head of what they want to be told though, is still really interesting to me. Regardless of the level of trauma, or pain, or just how lost someone might be in life, they still want to be told what they want to be told.

How many times do you suppose people ask for advice with a preferred answer or response already in their head?

Well, you don't have to suppose because I already surveyed a few thousand people to ask them. My survey consisted of just three questions:

1. When you ask someone for advice, do you generally already have an idea of what you want to hear from them in their response?

2. How often do you get the response you were hoping to hear?

3. If you didn't get the advice you wanted to hear, how likely are you to take that advice?

Of the 1,874 people who responded, 82.3% of people confirmed that when they asked for advice, they already had something in mind that they were wanting to hear back.

Interestingly, in almost three out of four times (73.4%), the person asking someone for advice was told exactly what they wanted to hear anyway.

And perhaps unsurprisingly, the overwhelming response to the third question as to what they did with the advice that they didn't want to hear, 78.8% of respondents said they were 'unlikely' or 'very unlikely' to take that advice.

In other words, advice is useless because people already know what they want to hear, and nobody listens to advice unless they were already thinking it themselves.

You've got to wonder, why do people ask for advice then?

―――――――――――――――― . ――――――――――――――――

You are just telling them what most other people are telling them anyway.

So, if the majority of us ask for advice with our preferred answer of that advice already in mind, and if the majority of us won't *take* advice unless it matches what we want to hear, you can probably accurately predict that every person you ask will probably tell you the same thing.

This is because of a phenomenon known as The Contingent Weighting Model.

See, humans are pretty simple animals.

We almost always prefer the road of least resistance.

The technical way of describing this decision-making process, is that our brains develop a hierarchy of models in which the trade-off between attributes is contingent on the nature of the response[28].

This leads to most people, when asked for advice, wrongly taking the asker's preferences into account and giving them that option, because we know that if we advise differently, they won't take our advice.

---

[28] Tversky, A., Sattath, S., & Slovic, P. (1988). Contingent weighting in judgment and choice. Psychological Review, 95, 371-384.

Importantly, studies have also shown that they are much less likely to ask for our advice again in the future[29].

And we've already established: we *love* being asked for advice.

Think about it: how often have you asked someone for advice in your life, and when they haven't told you exactly what you wanted to hear, you put them down a few spots in the hierarchy of people you ask for advice in the future?

Some people counter this by saying, yes but they have been there before, or they are experts in this subject, or they are really successful people, so why wouldn't I ask them for advice?

But that's the reason!

A study published this year[30] showed that just because someone is successful or knowledgeable or an expert in a particular topic, the advice they give is basically no more beneficial than the advice that anyone else gives.

Unexpected, right?

[29] Kray LJ. (2000). Contingent Weighting in Self-Other Decision Making. Organic Behavioural Human Decision Processes, 83(1), 82-106.

[30] Levari DE, Gilbert DT, Wilson TD. (2022). Tips From the Top: Do the Best Performers Really Give the Best Advice? Psychological Science, 33(5):685-698.

Perhaps less unexpected though, is that even when that result was shown to people, they *still* believed the 'successful' person's advice was better.

Why?

Turns out, it's because, even though the successful person doesn't give better advice, they just give more of it.

And unfortunately, when it comes to advice, humans seem to favour quantity over quality.

I think this just further illustrates the futility of asking for advice. If someone is only going to tell me what I want to hear, and if everyone is basically the same in that way, why would I bother?

_____ · _____

It gets you entwined.

Another reason why I think we should steer clear of giving advice is that, let's face it, sometimes it's just better not to get involved.

When we give advice about a particular situation, we are then tied to the outcome of the situation forever more.

Chances are you are not as socially awkward or uncomfortable as I am, but I have been in the situation – horribly more than once – where my mate has asked for my advice about a particular girl after they have broken up. I have told him what I thought of her, and then they end up getting married, and every single social situation after that is even more weird and awkward.

You would think I would have learned not to get involved, and I hope I have, but you never know.

———————————————— · ————————————————

You don't have to deal with the fallout.

On the other hand, of course, when you ask someone for advice, and they happily give you it, they are also sometimes completely free from dealing with any consequences of it.

They don't have to pick up the pieces if the advice they give you somehow blows up or blows your life up.

They don't have to be part of the break-up conversation that they have actually initiated with their advice to you.

They don't have to be sit in the cubicle in your safe job in your safe business in your safe life that you chose – based on their advice – against the opportunity they had to leave that career and start their own business.

They are in the enviable position of just being able to declare their hand, tell you what you should do, and then disappear while you do it.

Turns out, it's much easier to give advice than to be held accountable for it.

Now this might sound perfect for you as an advice-giver: all care and no responsibility.

But if you are someone who is motivated by giving advice to someone while knowing that you are not going to have to be around to see what happens afterwards, maybe you are not the best person to be telling them what to do.

––––––––––––––––––––––––– . –––––––––––––––––––––––––

We are much better at being sympathetic when someone loses, than being happy when someone wins.

And this matters because it makes advice-givers are lot more cautious and conservative in their advice to others, compared to what they would do themselves in the same situation.

Jason Dana and Daylian Cain from the Yale School of Management conducted some studies[31] into this phenomenon and found that "decision-makers are significantly more risk-averse when choosing for others than when choosing for themselves."

They found a number of reasons for this.

"First", they wrote, "people appear to have a limited capacity for symhedonia – positive feelings about others' good fortune.

People are instead more sympathetic to others' losses.

Advisers may thus be prone to weighing losses more heavily than gains when making choices for, or offering advice to others."

Accountability was another factor that influenced advice-givers they found.

---

[31] Dana, J., & Cain, D. M. (2015). Advice versus choice. Current Opinion in Psychology, 6, 173-176.

"Advisers also expect to be held accountable for any advice they give. While this accountability has self-evident benefits, people tend to be blamed for failure more than they are credited for success.

Fully aware of this imbalance, advisers will likely give more weight to a decision's potential negative fallout than its potential benefits."

The researchers found that this creates a bigger problem: when the aim of a policy is to improve the quality of advice, it can unintentionally end up making everything worse!

If advice-givers feel more accountable, they are likely to be even more risk-averse, making them less likely to give riskier advice, even if it's better advice.

Likewise, if advice-givers are too close or have a deep personal connection with the person they are advising, they are more likely to be more cautious and more compliant, and simply more likely to just tell people what they want to hear.

———————————————— · ————————————————

Which advice have you actually remembered? And which advice have you actually taken?

This is the great test of it all.

When you ask someone to recall the best bit of advice they ever got, they invariably answer with something like, "pursue your dreams", "follow your passion", "save money" or "buy a house", and "never give up".

OK, they might all be great bits of advice, but are you just reciting those bits of advice because you were really given them, or just because they are the same bits of advice that everyone gives/gets?

And then apply the second test, can you think of the best advice you were given *and* recall the person who gave you it?

Chances are you might recall one, maybe two, pieces of advice that you think was really helpful in your life, and they might have been given to you by one, or maybe two, different people.

Now, contrast that with just how many pieces of advice you have been given in your life, and how many people have given you it.

One or two gems amongst maybe hundreds of people telling you how to do something, why to do something, and what not to do?

Those number just don't stack up.

But isn't therapy advice?

I am what's called a 'non-directional therapist'[32]

That means if you engage in therapy with me, the sessions are pretty much all about you and your story. It doesn't mean that the therapy has no direction, it just means that the direction of the therapy always comes from the client, not from me.

That's because I, and all of the other non-directional therapists, believe that giving advice isn't a therapist's job. I think giving advice can hold a client back from recovery and growth. I think that it just replaces their confused story of lived experience with *my* confused story of lived experience.

How is that helping?

In 2020, a bunch of psychology researchers from the University of Maryland[33] found that not only was advice in therapy a bad idea, but it usually said a lot more about the anxiety and neediness of the therapist than it did about the client asking for and receiving the therapist's advice.

---

[32] Non-Directional Therapy, also called client-centred or person-centred psychotherapy, an approach to the treatment of mental disorders that aims primarily toward fostering personality growth by helping individuals gain insight into and acceptance of their feelings, values, and behaviour (Britannica).

[33] Prass, M., Ewell, A., Hill, C. E., & Kivlighan Jr, D. M. (2021). Solicited and Unsolicited Therapist Advice inPsychodynamic Psychotherapy: Is it Advised?. Counselling Psychology Quarterly, 34(2), 253-274.

Some schools of therapy, for instance behavioural therapy, hold advice giving as a mainstay of how they work with clients[34]. Behavioural therapy clients say that the two things that are helpful in therapy is talking to someone who understands their situation and understands them, and getting advice[35].

Family therapy is another area where therapists are trained, and encouraged, to give advice to their clients (a big reason why I'm not a family therapist).

They believe that professionals know what's best for the family, and of course the family doesn't know what's best for themselves.

These therapists would say that *they* should take responsibility and make decisions for people, because clearly if they are sitting across from them, people can't take responsibility for finding solutions themselves.

And mostly, they believe that families want advice, they benefit from advice, and when they give families advice, they take it.

The arrogance of that is frankly astounding.

But are the therapists just responding to what their clients say they want, and in the interest of

[34] Silver, E. (1991). Should I give advice? A systemic view. Journal of Family Therapy, 13, 295-309.

[35] Murphy, P. M., Crame, D., and Lillie, F. J. (1984). The relationship between curative factors perceived by patients in their psychotherapy and treatment outcome: an exploratory study. British Journal of Medical Psychology, 57, 187-192.

keeping them as clients and keeping their business alive, they just go with it?

Over 50 years ago, psychiatric patients were surveyed and the majority of them said that they expected to get some advice from their therapist and would come away from their session disappointed if they didn't get it[36]. More recently, psychology clients still value advice from their therapists and the absence of advice is described as 'unhelpful' or 'uncaring'[37].

But I don't know, something about that just doesn't sit right with me.

If a client is sitting across from a therapist because of their history of being controlled and manipulated and used, do they really benefit from then the same thing being perpetrated by their therapist?

And, once again, does the therapist know everything there is to know about the client, the other actors in the client's story, and their situation and history?

Look, I've been receiving therapy for a long, long time, and there are still quite a few things that my therapist doesn't know about me because I haven't told him yet.

---

[36] Goin, M. K., Yamamoto, J. & Silverman, J. (1965). Therapy congruent with class linked expectations. Archives of General Psychiatry, 13, 133-137.

[37] Dryden, W. (1989) Key Issues for Counselling in Action. London: Sage.

If he was an advice-giving therapist (which thankfully he isn't), he would be giving that advice without really knowing the intricacies of the situations he was advising on.

And I doubt he would be the only one.

Is a therapist who gives advice rather than therapy, actually not a therapist, but a teacher?

I think that distinction has to be made, your therapist is either providing therapy, or they are a teacher providing *education*.

Which is fine, but let's call it what it is then.

In a famous family therapy book[38] published in the 80's, the authors wrote:

If you're not neutral, you give instructions and advice, you tell people what to do and what not to do.
Then you are an educator, not a therapist.
The world needs teachers and preachers and policemen and parents to distinguish between what is good and bad, useful and not useful, but a therapist should not fall into that category.

---

[38] Boscolo, L., Cecchin, G., Hoffman, L., & Penn, P. (1987). Milan Systemic Family Therapy. New York: Basic Books.

I couldn't agree more.

The truth is, therapists like me don't do advice, we do therapy.

A lot of my clients wish that it wasn't that way. They would really prefer not to do the hard work on themselves, and put themselves through hours of therapy to come to a decision. They would much rather I – or anyone really – would just tell them what to do.

But it's not how it works.

As the psychologist, Claire Newton[39], writes, "how could anyone arrive, give the psychologist a broad overview of the issue that is troubling them and expect to be told what to do to fix it all within a typical 50-to-60-minute consultation?

It's unrealistic, especially when the issue is probably complicated, involves patterns of thinking and behaviour that have been a lifetime in the making and are probably unconscious or out of the individual's awareness, entangled to many different elements of the individual's life, and wrapped up in painful and difficult emotions which the client may not want to even admit to, let alone deal with."

Newton puts it simply: anyone can give advice, but only psychotherapists can do psychotherapy.

---

[39] https://www.clairenewton.co.za/my-articles/giving-advice-versus-psychotherapy.html

To give advice requires no skill, but therapy requires specific and complex skills, that are difficult to learn and take time. Advice is one-way communication, where (good) therapy is two-way.

Advice gives direction, where therapy is non-directive.

And, importantly, advice is unlikely to change a person's behaviour, where therapy is conclusively shown to change someone's behaviour, and that behaviour change is usually deep and long-lasting.

I am glad I paid so little attention to good advice, had I abided by it I might have been saved from some of my most valuable mistakes.

Edna St. Vincent Millay

CHAPTER 4:

Some of the best advice
I've ever been given.

Surely *all* advice doesn't suck ... right?

Well, no. I mean I have received some good advice in my life. Here, I will list them.

1. When you get pregnant with your first child, don't listen to anyone else's advice or stories about their pregnancy, labour, and birth. They will only tell you the horror stories that they've either been through, or their mum's neighbour's sister went through.

2. Move every day. It doesn't have to be a marathon. Get up. Get dressed. Go outside. And move.

3. Don't mow the grass in bare feet.

That's it really.

CHAPTER 5:

Some of the suckiest
advice ever given.

OK, if you are still with me, this is where I might lose you because so many of these crappy bits of advice are given out by ALL of us ALL the time.

The thing is, a lot of these are used so often and so widely by people that they don't even seem like advice anymore.

They have somehow just become part of our vernacular.

And while they might seem like throwaway lines and not really that important or impactful, for a lot of people who are vulnerable, or upset, or lacking in esteem, they can be *very* impactful.

A lot of this terrible advice comes from WMAG's, and often they pass it on to someone else without ever having really thought about it, but just because someone they love said it to them once (or a million times).

So, let's look a bit deeper into some of the suckiest advice ever, who gives it, what situation they give it in (often the wrong one), and then why that person is giving it, and what they probably really mean.

See how many of these you can tick off as either something you have said, or something that has been said to you.

Follow your passion.

You are usually told to "follow your passion" by WMAGs who have not followed theirs.

This advice is largely given to young people who haven't realised how disappointing the world can be compared to the relative shelter of living at home and being told how awesome and pretty and clever you are for your entire life.

And sometimes to new divorcees.

It can be loosely translated to: "Don't get stuck in a crappy job/marriage/home/relationship/town like I have, do something different and take a bit of a risk". Not a terrible theme to be honest, but it can also be a bit of a happiness trap.

Being told to follow your passion is responsible for a whole lot of people actually not finding anything because they waste so much of their time, money, and their life's effort searching for that one thing they are truly passionate about.

And for a lot of people, that's a waste of time.

In truth, passion isn't something that's out there somewhere just waiting for you to stumble across it.

It's something that we build and grow and develop. It's something we realise we have after doing something similar for a long time.

Someone who really loves home renovating becomes passionate about paint colours and cushions.

Someone who really loves basketball becomes passionate about coaching kids' basketball.

Someone who likes to listen to people's stories and their struggles becomes passionate about psychology or social work.

These passions weren't in us all the time, we grew them.

There's also the inference that we are only useful or good at something if we are also passionate about it. Rubbish.

Mike Rowe is a television presenter famous for his Discovery Channel show, Dirty Jobs, where he takes a deep dive (sometimes disgustingly literally) into some of the weirdest, messiest and smelliest occupations in the world.

He speaks to a lot of people who seem to love their disgusting job, and some who are quite passionate about it, and he often tries to answer the question: why would anyone do this job?

Could it be passion? Could they just have realised they are really good at it? And is being passionate and being good at it somehow linked? Rowe doesn't think so.

"Just because you're passionate about something doesn't mean you won't suck at it", Rowe said. "And just because you're determined to improve doesn't mean that you will. Does that mean you shouldn't pursue a thing you're passionate about? Of course not. The question is, for how long, and to what end?"

After all of the weird and wonderful jobs that Rowe has seen people do, would he recommend that people always follow their passion when it comes to their work? "I would never advise that until I understand who they are, what they want, and why they want it", he says. "Even then, I'd be cautious. Passion is too important to be without, but too fickle to be guided by."

If we are not following our passion, or worse, if we don't even feel like we have one, we can also feel less-than, or that we are somehow not trying hard enough to find the right path.

Not everyone needs, or has, a passion. I know a few people who are fortunate enough to have a few of them.

People who have built careers and businesses on the back of something they had become really passionate about. People who found out after mucking their way through a whole lot of other stuff they didn't love before they put their head down and really worked on one of the things they felt a great affinity to.

But that's not the norm. Think about it: how many people do you know in your life who consistently do something they are really passionate about, much less have made a career or built a business around it?

It's also worth considering if we only think of something being our passion if we also find it 'fun'. Can we be passionate about something if it doesn't necessarily bring us limitless joy and fun?

In 2017, some researchers at Harvard University analysed the graduation speeches given to students over the last decade at the top 100 universities[40]. A lot of these speeches, unsurprisingly, included the speaker giving the students advice on how to 'follow their passion'.

"Much of the advice centred on "focusing on what you love" as the way to follow your passion", the researchers found. "But some speakers described the pursuit of passion as "focusing on what you care about". The distinction is subtle but meaningful: focusing on what you love associates passion with what you enjoy, and what makes you happy, whereas focusing on what you care about aligns passion with your values and the impact you want to have".

What difference does that make?

---

[40] Jachimowicz, J., Guenoun, B., To, C., Menges, J., & Akinola, M. (2017, December 7). Pursuing Passion through Feelings or Values: How Lay Beliefs Guide the Pursuit of Passion.

Well, the researchers found that when people pursued something they cared about more than something that they thought was fun, it helped them stay the course and reach their goals.

"Consider that the German word for passion, "Leidenschaft", literally translates to "the ability to suffer hardship", the researchers wrote. "Passion alone is only weakly related to employees' performance at their work. But the combination of passion and perseverance – i.e., the extent to which employees stick with their goals even in the face of adversity – was related to higher performance".

They also pointed out that "passion wanes over time", so if somebody is focused only on what makes them happy, they are less likely to persevere through hard times than if they were focused on something that they actually really care about.

~~Follow your passion~~.

Focus on what you care about.

———————————— · ————————————

Never give up.

This piece of crap advice is usually given by somebody who has, indeed, given up.

They say it to you when they don't want to crush your dream, even when they secretly believe your dream might not be possible. And it's almost always a reflection of their experience, and their own surrender.

"Don't do what I did. I quit, and now I'm in this place. And it's rubbish".

This is one that we would have all heard a lot. And, in the right context, it's not terrible advice.

In the rehab facility where I started my recovery, there was a sign that said 'don't give up before the miracle happens'. In that situation, it was absolutely golden advice.

The trouble is, for a lot of people, they will stick at a situation, stuck in that situation, just *in case* the miracle happens: their partner will start treating them better, their adult son will stop using heroin, their asshole boss will finally realise how invaluable they are.

And while they are waiting for those things to happen, their hearts – and their lives – are dying.

In my previous life as a business coach and now as a therapist, I have come across loads of people who were hanging on for dear life but in fact, letting go and 'giving up' would have made a lot more sense for them.

A small business owner whose business was in printing, ink cartridges, and copying, who flatly refused to concede that the world was changing and his product offering was less and less necessary every year.

Another small business guy who still maintained that people would always want to keep something on a DVD (which his business did for customers) despite everyone in the world saying "no thanks, I will just upload it to the cloud".

A wife who had been telling me for almost seven years that her partner was going to stop drinking and start focusing more on her and their children, despite the overwhelming evidence that he had no intention of doing that.

If giving up is so hard when the evidence supporting the decision is so obvious, how are we supposed to navigate the more subtle circumstances in which giving up would be beneficial but less obvious to us?

The thing that makes ending something and starting something else hard is the stigma that society attaches to it. Even the phrase 'giving up' sounds so weak and dismissive.

But the world is full of examples where it's been made better because somebody 'gave up'.

Mark Zuckerberg may not have created Facebook if he hadn't dropped out of Harvard to build the company.

The same can be said of Google, whose founders Larry Page and Sergey Brin also dropped out of college, this time Stanford University.

Bill Gates and Steve Jobs did the same.

Another Stanford alumnus, John McEnroe might never have become one of the greatest athletes ever if he hadn't given up college.

And what if Beyoncé had never pursued her solo career?

Sometimes the absolute best option is to give up. Sometimes, not always. When you realise you don't want the thing you are pursuing so hard as much as you used to.

When chasing that thing is making you unhappy, making you lose contact and connection with people that matter to you, or when you finally come to the realisation that it's just not going to work out how you want it to.

It might require you to reframe 'giving up' into something a bit more kind to yourself: 'I'm going to stop pursuing *that* thing so I have the space to start focusing on a *new* thing'.

Don't just cut and run.

Take an inventory of everything you have learned and any value you can take from what you have tried, and maybe apply it to the next pursuit.

But in the end, as my boy Kenny sang, "you gotta know when to hold 'em, and know when to fold 'em".

~~Never give up~~.

Never stop trying to find happiness.

—————————— · ——————————

Be strong.

I hate it when people say this.

It's said by someone who doesn't have any feelings out loud or visible, and would prefer it if you didn't either.

Usually, it's when Person A has been through something big and heavy and emotional (death of a loved one, loss of a job, life-threatening diagnosis) and Person B is being told about the tragedy, but is emotionally ill-equipped to deal with it.

When someone tells another person to "be strong", often what they mean is "please don't outwardly show me any emotion or upset, because if you do, I might have to also feel something emotional, and I have trained my brain to hide and run from all of that stuff. So, if it's OK with you, just keep your sadness and your grief and emotion to yourself and ... be strong".

This is also the classic example of a situation where someone is sharing something difficult from their life with someone else, and instead of just listening to them and showing empathy and being with them, we feel compelled to say something – anything – and 'be strong' is the best we can come up with.

Not to mention the fact that it also says to Person A that they are, right now, *not* being strong and they could be doing better at that. It doesn't say "continue to be strong" or "I'm so impressed with how strong you are being", it's much more of a direction, or an order.

"Be strong will you?"

"If you could be strong, you could get through this easier ... basically, you need to be more like me and less like you right now."

"Right now ... you're being kind of weak".

Don't you think that if that person had the facility of strength in this moment they would be using it? They have just been through something big and potentially life-changing, they didn't ask you to appraise their strength or their ability to cope with that change.

The problem is that a lot of people hear a lot of people saying this crap, and when they face some adversity it's the thing they remember. So, they try to be strong. They bottle shit up. They push it way down. And it makes them sick, and their pain worse.

It's OK to be sad. You are allowed to feel shit and you don't have to pretend like you're not. You don't have to be anything. For anyone.

There's no way around this one: if you tell someone to be strong, you are also telling them that they're not. And given they are probably struggling through something pretty heavy at that moment, maybe you should keep your crap advice to yourself?

~~Be strong.~~ Be whatever you are, whenever you are it.

———————————— . ————————————

You're over-reacting.

I've always found the best way to stop someone from over-reacting to something is to calmly inform them that they are, in fact, over-reacting.

Works every time.

The arrogance of this one is pretty amazing. People who tell you not to over-react have also been told never to over-react to anything. Either that, or they are someone who thinks *any* reaction is an over-reaction, especially if it doesn't match their own.

The context here is that you are upset or annoyed at something you perceive to be an injustice.

The WMAG doesn't care that that's how you feel, because you should in fact be feeling something else altogether (and they are happy to tell you what that is too).

They might say "You react in an overly dramatic way to everything", but what they mean is "your feelings aren't important or valid."

In some situations, a person's reaction to what is happening might be the only thing they can actually control, the only thing they can take ownership of. And when you think about it, everyone's reaction to a particular situation is *their* reaction, it doesn't have to match anyone else's, it doesn't have to be anything at all.

I think people are entitled to their own truths, and to their own reactions when they feel one of their boundaries has been violated. When we tell someone that their emotions are inappropriate, we are exerting a sense of control over that person that can be harmful and damaging in other areas of their life as well. We are telling them that what they feel is wrong. That *they* are wrong.

But are they wrong? Or is over-reacting not only normal, but necessary?

Reacting to a threat is a normal thing that humans have evolved to understand being something that keeps us safe.

Therefore, over-reacting just means this particular threat is greater.

The thing is, we are all allowed to determine what our own threats are, and how severe they are.

Something might not feel like much of a threat to you, but for someone else, it might be crippling.

The writer, Gillian Brown[41], also points out that telling someone they are over-reacting is one of the tools that a narcissist will use to control and gaslight someone else.

She writes: "Accusing a person or a group of people of 'overreacting' is a commonly used silencing

_____

[41] thebodyisnotanapology.com

tactic. Indeed, it is used so often by people in positions of privilege (politicians, the rich, white men, abusers, and anybody else who likes to frequently tell others to 'just calm down') towards the less privileged (minority groups, activist groups, victims of abuse, etc) that it has practically become cliché. It is an effective silencing tactic, because it paints the accused as ridiculous, hysterical, and not to be taken seriously. But when you are asking for what you need, you are not being ridiculous and hysterical. They, whether consciously or unconsciously, are being controlling and manipulative. They are in the wrong, not you."

~~You're overacting.~~

You're feeling something.

———————————————— · ————————————————

Good things come to those who wait.

There are two options for this little gem to be used:

(1) the person who uses passive patience to sit and wait for something magical to happen to them instead of working for it (and hopes that you will too so as to not one-up them), or

(2) someone who is tired of listening to you go on and on about your dream, and is trying to shut you up about it.

The situation is usually when someone is impatient and wants to achieve something a lot quicker than other people might think is the right amount of time to have achieved it.

The translation?

Slow down. Be patient. Oh, and don't get out of your lane or want something too hard because then it might shine a light on me and my sitting around endlessly waiting for a miracle and it never happening.

First of all, is this statement even true?

Do good things only happen to people who are patient and wait for them?

Let's use my son as an example here. He has two choices. He can wait until I offer him a brownie I have just baked, or he can just go and grab one. In this context the good thing (the brownie) didn't come to him through waiting, it came to him because he is resourceful and has been taught to have his needs met.

Secondly then, how many people do you know who have waited and waited and waited in the wrong job for them, or with the wrong person for them, or in the wrong place for them, and never seemed to have anything good come to them?

I know so many people in that particular rut.

When are their good things coming?

Should they hang around a bit longer?

Does waiting and waiting make them more likely? Or more deserving?

This could be reframed from 'good things come to those who wait' to 'good things come when you have the awareness of what is good for you, you know how to achieve it, you work hard and put in the right amount of effort to achieve it, and then you are grateful for it once you have achieved it.

That's a bit wordy though.

Also, if good things come only to those who wait ages for them to come, that thing you think is a good thing in your life that you didn't have to toil and sacrifice and wait for? This person reckons it's not. The more you think about it, this one just sounds like crap advice from a bitter person who hasn't received the things in life they think they deserve but is still waiting. Miserably.

Oh, one more thing. "Good things come to those who wait" is not even the full quote. Abraham Lincoln actually said, "Good things come to those who wait, but only the things left by those who hustle."

———————————————— · ————————————————

You are perfect just the way you are.

Usually said to you by your parents when you start going through puberty and you become a sad, and moody, hairy and distorted version of your previous cute self.

Also by your supportive friends who really want you to date again after your horror break-up because they don't want you to stay on their couch any longer.

It is used in the context of 'if someone can't see how great you are, that's on them'. Not terrible messaging to be honest.

When it's used in the supportive sense, it means that "even with your faults and flaws, I still think you are pretty great".

In the slightly more cynical sense, it could also mean, "please don't keep working on yourself because I have always enjoyed my superiority over you, and if you keep growing that might be in jeopardy".

In truth, the best we can hope for is to be 'perfectly imperfect'.

That state of being flawed and, well ... human, but also totally enough for someone else and for ourselves while in that state.

After all, perfection is an end-point right?

I mean, it's the ultimate end-point really.

Nothing can be better than it. There is literally no growth past it. You can't be better than perfect. Perfect just ... is.

I think we can benefit more from growing and actually wanting to keep growing and learning and getting better.

I don't want perfection, but the striving towards perfection is a pretty good use of my time I reckon.

————————————— · —————————————

You can do anything you put your mind to.

No. You can't.

This is said to you by your parents, when you are still too young to know that this is one of the silliest things people say.

Child:

"I want to [be invisible/fly/shoot
webs from my wrists/live on the sun/eat
nothing but caramel]."

Parent:

"You can do anything you put
your mind to Sweetheart".

Child:

"Really?"

Parent:

"No."

Someone shares their life goals with someone else. That person, instead of explaining what the odds of their goal being achieved (without completely disintegrating them and causing them to abandon their ambition), and how much work might be involved in reaching them, gives them a false affirmation that they can do anything, they just have to put their mind to it.

The translation?

"You can't do that, but I don't want to be the one to crush your dreams, let the rest of the world do that once your hopes are really up."

Not everyone can be what somebody else is, or what someone else has achieved.

And not everyone needs to.

There's a reason only 12 people have walked on the moon, and only about 500 people have ever been to space.

It's hard. And it's limited.

One of the reasons there are so many failed tech startups[42] and so many injuries of kids thinking they are able to fly[43], is that not enough people are told when

---

[42] According to Investopedia, in 2019, the failure rate of startups was around 90%. Research concludes 21.5% of startups fail in the first year, 30% in the second year, 50% in the fifth year, and 70% in their 10th year.

[43] A 2007 study in the prestigious paediatric medicine journal, Archives of Disease in Childhood, even showed that kids were even more likely to be injured jumping off roofs and out of trees when they were wearing superhero costumes. [Davies,

they are young that dreams require work, not everything is for everybody, and also ... physics.

I know, I know, it sounds like I am a miserable dream-crusher but that's not true at all.

I love dreams.

I love a pursuit that seems unattainable but for which I will still work hard and chase.

I just also know there are limits to what I can do and be, and no advice in the world will change that.

———————————————— · ————————————————

Surridge, Hole, & Munro-Davies (2007). Superhero-related injuries in paediatrics: a case series. Archives of Disease in Childhood, 92(3), 242-243.

Success is a journey, not a destination.

Delivered by someone who doesn't think you will reach your dream, or who has no direction in their own life and wants some company.

Or when you are working hard towards something, and it seems like you might have to change and try something new, but someone else really wants you to stay where you are, and instead enjoy the struggle somehow.

They are confusingly saying: no matter what you do, as long as you keep holding on doggedly to your ambition and as long as you try, you can't fail.

If you want to win the lottery, it seems to me that you might consider success to be when the lottery winnings end up in your bank account, and not the thousands of tickets you had to buy over the years trying to win it.

Sales expert, Grant Cardone[44] says that success isn't a journey, it is the state that you control and have responsibility over.

"No NFL club tells their fan base that it's the journey that counts.

Everyone knows it's all about the ring: the Super Bowl.

---

[44] www.grantcardone.com

A fireman driving a fire truck isn't focused on the journey, he's focused on getting to the fire and putting it out.

Your life is no different.

It's the destination that matters most.

People who say otherwise are likely running a seminar or trying to sell a book.[45]

---

[45] Well, this is awkward.

When you encounter seemingly good advice that contradicts other seemingly good advice, ignore them both.

Al Franken

Just be positive.

The giver of this advice is that particular WMAG who also sweeps everything hard or confrontational under the metaphorical rug.

You have sought out someone to validate your feelings, listen to your problems, and maybe show some empathy.

Instead, you found someone who would prefer you just to smile and fake happiness for their sake.

It's not all about you, you know.

What they are really saying? "Your whining is really starting to annoy me now."

If we have no chronic mental health disturbance, when we are not feeling positive, it's usually for a good reason.

It helps us sense when we are in danger, or when we need help and support, and when someone else is potentially violating one of our boundaries.

It keeps us, and our mental health, safe.

And for people who do have a chronic mental health condition that affects their positivity like clinical depression, to be told to "just be positive" is as helpful as being told to "just grow another arm".

As Australian speaker and coach, Michael Johnson[46] writes, neither life nor people are always positive or always negative, and to hope for balance might be more helpful.

"If a person is overly optimistic", Johnson writes, "they usually don't consider the risks associated with their actions or learn through painful trial and error.

Many self-proclaimed 'positive thinkers' beat themselves up internally for their negative thoughts while setting unrealistic expectations about constantly feeling happy or peaceful. It's better to stay balanced: there's a time and place for all emotions."

I can't argue with that.

---

[46] www.themojomaster.com.au

Fake it 'til you make it.

Ironically, this advice is usually given by someone who has never done either.

Think about the situation where you are offered a job that you are neither qualified for, or able to do. Instead of being honest and authentic and saying, "I am really flattered to be offered this job, but I have absolutely no idea what I am doing", this terrible advice suggests you instead lie and bumble your way through it until you either learn how to do it properly, or get fired for lying in the first place.

As James Sudakow[47] writes, honesty and authenticity will usually win out anyway.

"The first time I got promoted into a leadership role", he wrote, "I wasn't sure I could do the job. Many leaders told me this advice (fake it till you make it). Whereas I understood what they were trying to say, I chose a different path – full transparency.

After working with employees at all levels throughout my career, I have found that people have really good BS detectors.

Lack of knowledge and experience can be forgiven and even embraced as signs of a humble leader.

---

[47] @jamessudakow

Lack of perceived authenticity often isn't.

I chose to be honest about what I knew and didn't know.

I found that it made people follow me more and help me be a successful leader."

Also, this one reeks of privilege.

Most people don't find themselves in a position where someone offers them a job that they are not qualified for, and that they will have to lie and fake their way through to get away with it.

Most people have to actually work really hard, and have a fair bit of luck and timing on their side to even be offered jobs that they are actually qualified for.

And it's not just professionally that this is a particularly terrible bit of advice.

I think that any advice that tells you to be sneaky and dishonest, as opposed to upfront and genuine, might not be very good advice.

I'll leave the final word on this one to Atomic Habits author, James Clear[48], who said that 'fake it till you make it' asks you to believe and invest in something about yourself with any evidence to support your ability to do it.

---

[48] @JamesClear

"We have a word for believing something without any evidence", Clear said, "it's called delusion".

———————————— · ————————————

If you love what you do, you'll never work a day in your life.

Occasionally in our lives we meet someone who has been lucky enough to find something they enjoy doing, and then they have worked out how to get paid for it too.

At the same time, you might tell them about the job that you hate and feel stuck in, hoping they will listen and maybe even offer you some empathy.

Instead, they give you this waffle.

They say to you, "you just have to find something that you love and you will never need a holiday and you will be thrilled every day of it".

But what they are really saying is "you are inferior to me because you don't emphatically love what you do for a job every minute of the day". Also, "all work is unenjoyable ... except mine".

How many people really enjoy their job? I mean, *really* enjoy it.

Like, they love going to work, and there isn't a single facet of their work that they find tedious or frustrating.

I can honestly say that I don't know *anyone* like that.

Every job, even the most enjoyable and fun ones have something: paperwork, people, governance, travel, people ... something that makes it not completely and utterly lovable.

A few friends of mine are professional athletes. From the outside, you wouldn't think you could imagine a better job and a better life. But all of them describe what they do as 'work', as in "I can't come to that thing because I've got to work". What they mean is, I have to train, or I have to travel to a game, or I am playing that day in another city or whatever, but to them it's still *work*.

More personally though, I can actually honestly say that I love what I do for work. Mostly.

Being a therapist and doing a bit of writing here and there is pretty great, really. But there are definitely parts of both jobs that I would happily give up if I could.

I hate admin, and I'm crap at it.

I don't love travelling for work.

I don't like some of the tech I have to use to deliver therapy remotely these days.

And while I love being a writer, and I love having written things, and seeing my books on book shop shelves, the actual process of writing isn't something I find all that much fun either.

People I have spoken to me who, like me, have started and run their own businesses all say the same thing too: you will never work as hard as you will work for yourself. And I think the same is true about a job or a business that you love.

The Danish community strategist, Trine Ravnkilde Frederiksen agrees.

"It's more like this: if you love what you do, you'll kinda work all the time", she writes. "I'm not saying work is bad, but if you keep chasing a work life that is nothing but fun and easy all the time, you're going to miss out on some amazing opportunities and lessons.

Work can be tough, weird, difficult, complicated, beautiful, fun, easy all at the same time! If you take every little bump in the road as a sign you're going in the wrong direction, you'll never get very far."

—————————————— · ——————————————

Stop playing the victim.

What does someone mean when they say this?

Are they saying that nothing (or nothing *that* bad) has happened to you so you should stop whinging and harping on about it?

Or are they saying that, OK, something did happen to you, but you don't have to keep going on about it still?

I hate hearing this sentence uttered because it makes me feel a bit envious. Anyone who tells someone else to not play the victim has clearly never been one.

And I'm jealous of them.

Worse, they are alluding to someone's trauma not actually being real.

As someone who has had their own abuse and trauma both discounted and actually flat out disbelieved (before it was proven indisputably), that really annoys me.

When someone has been abused, and therefore is a victim, someone else can manipulate them, put them down, or just outright bully them, victimising them even more than the original abuse.

That starts with someone telling them not to 'play the victim'.

Well, that's easy for someone to say who isn't a victim. The only people who tell you not to 'play the victim' are bullies.

When I wasn't mentally well, and someone told me that I was playing the victim, in my vulnerability at the time I was confused.

Was that what I was doing?

Was I consciously doing it?

Should I just get over it, or maybe just push it all back down inside?

Were they right?

Was my abuse not that bad after all?

Now that I am mentally well, I would react very differently. Because now if someone tells me I am playing the victim, I would simply respond that yes, I probably am. And there's a really good reason for that: I *am* a victim.

There's no way I am going to let someone without empathy or kindness take my life experience from me.

There's no way I am going to let someone dilute the pain and sadness that I felt, and continue to feel, over what happened to me.

How dare they even try?

I didn't ask to be abused. I didn't ask for the trauma to still exist in my head as PTSD. I am, in every sense of the word, a victim.

So yes, I think this is crap advice, and basically a crap thing to say to someone.

Be better.

Be kind.

They are just being an attention-seeker.

I often hear this from my therapy clients who are, or have been, experiencing suicidal thoughts and told someone – usually in their family – about it.

They are told that are just being attention-seekers.

Stop being a drama queen.

Suck it up.

Be a man, etc etc.

You might hear this advice from someone when you tell them that you are worried about someone else who might be suicidal.

Or at least going through some difficult stuff and posting about it on Facebook.

Or honestly letting you into their life for a moment.

"They are just an attention-seeker, ignore them."

The thing is ... they're right.

That person making the "cry for help" are probably doing just that: asking for help.

There is a difference between attention-seeking and attention-*needing*.

And when someone is needing attention like that, the attention might be life-saving too.

How many people have needed attention, sought it from someone who decried them as an attention-seeker, and their isolation just got even worse?

Even unbearable?

———————————— · ————————————

Just say yes, and then work it out.

I don't know how you trust someone who gives you this advice.

Seems to me that this advice comes easily to someone for whom lying comes easily.

Much like 'fake it till you make it', this says if you don't know how to do something, just lie and say you do.

Someone giving this advice has obviously been untruthful about something before, felt no remorse about that, and now would love an accomplice in you.

It is most often attributed to a tweet by the billionaire entrepreneur Richard Branson[49] where he said: "if somebody offers you an amazing opportunity but you are not sure you can do it, say yes – then learn how to do it later!"

There's no way around it, the advice here is to be dishonest.

After that though, you are also making life much more difficult for yourself. It's hard enough doing stuff you know how to confidently do without also having to learn a whole new lot of skills.

---

[49] @richardbranson

Emma Hatto is the co-founder of Executive Recruitment startup, Bower.

She adds that lies are hard to keep up with.

"Sorry, I can't come to your third hen-do celebration this year, it's my Great-Aunt Dorothy's 80th birthday party".

If you've ever told a white lie, you'll know that over time, it grows arms and legs and somewhere down the line, you respond with 'who?' when your friend asks how Great-Aunt Dot's getting on", she wrote.

Telling lies in the professional setting as advocated by Richard Branson is almost always going to find you out, Hatto writes.

"When you're dishonest about your skills, it's going to come out in one way or another, probably sooner rather than later.

If you're just upfront and honest from the get-go, you can avoid a few very awkward conversations, a bruised reputation and a whole load of stress."

For another perspective, put yourself in the other position.

Somebody who is asking you if you can do something for them.

Something that probably means a lot to them. Something that they might have taken quite a while to get the courage up to ask you to do for them.

Them: "Can you do it for me?"

[In Your Mind]: OK, I don't know how to do it, but that doesn't matter. If I tell them I don't know how to do that, they might have more respect for me and show me how to do it, or at least give me the job anyway knowing that I might need some assistance myself to complete it. On the other hand, my ego is pretty fragile, and I prefer to have everyone think I can do anything, regardless of whether lying about this robs me of not only integrity but also my dignity.

Me: "Yep."

At the risk of getting a bit biblical, don't do something to someone that you wouldn't want done to you.

Lead with honesty. If nothing else, it's just so much easier.

———————————— · ————————————

Patience is a virtue.

This phrase has been around for a long time.

It first appeared in writing in a William Langland poem that he wrote in 1360, but its origin goes back even further to a fifth century poem that detailed vices (bad) and virtues (good) as two people fighting against each other.

So again, I am struck by the need for nostalgia in some people's life direction.

I'm not sure anyone in the 5th century had much insight into what the world would like that today, the challenges we would be facing, and the decisions we would have to make.

Yet some of us are still very ready to espouse life advice based on a poem written more than 1,700 years ago.

While it's a sweet notion: that if you are patient and wait your turn and not rock the boat, good things will happen to you, I actually think more often than not, the person dishing out this advice is really saying, "I am in no hurry to do anything ... and I would like some company."

You are entitled to your opinion.

Are you though?

As the Australian philosopher, Patrick Stokes[50], puts it: "You are not entitled to your opinion. You are only entitled to what you can argue for." The writer, Harlan Ellison[51] agrees, saying "You are not entitled to your opinion. You are entitled to your *informed* opinion. No one is entitled to be ignorant."

Opinions aren't facts.

Someone claiming their right to their opinion, however idiotic, or someone telling another person that they are entitled to their opinion because it's obviously not one they share, is just a pretty rudimentary way to stop a discussion, or to not let a discussion descend into an argument.

"The problem with 'I'm entitled to my opinion' is that, all too often, it's used to shelter beliefs that should have been abandoned", Stokes says.

"It becomes shorthand for 'I can say or think whatever I like' – and by extension, continuing to argue is somehow disrespectful.

And this attitude feeds, I suggest, into the false equivalence between experts and non-experts that is an

---

[50] @patstokes
[51] @harlanellison9

increasingly pernicious feature of our public discourse."[52]

This sense of entitlement also leads to people declaring that someone can believe what they want to believe.

But that's not really true either.

A friend of mine believes the Earth is flat. Another believes vaccinations don't work. (Ok look, I have a wide range of friends OK?).

Yet another friend says that he doesn't believe in gay marriage.

But surely, when stacked against an insurmountable amount of evidence – scientific evidence – that the first two 'beliefs' are absolutely wrong, and the third is just weird because I have at least three really good couple friends who are both married to each other and gay, their belief is just ... well, wrong.

So, are my friends not allowed to believe in those things?

Are they entitled to their opinion about the Earth being flat or my married gay friends being real?

The important factor here, I guess, is that while some of my friends have some pretty bonkers beliefs,

---

[52] https://theconversation.com/no-youre-not-entitled-to-your-opinion-9978

none of them have any political power, and most people think they are bonkers.

But recently the world has seen the ascension of some people who not only believe things that can't be proven (polite way of putting it), or just lie and compound other lies (the reality of it), this bit of advice suddenly becomes a bit more sinister and dangerous.

———————————— · ————————————

I'm living the dream.

How many people living on Earth right now do you honestly think are living the dream?

What does that even mean?

I love my life.

I love my kids.

I love my work.

I love where I live.

I am really, honestly, very grateful for all of that.

But is it my dream?

Well, I'm essentially a pretty lazy person, so my dream wouldn't include any work for a start.

So how do people deliver this sentence as advice (other than multi-level marketing 'managers' trying to sign you up to their pyramid scheme)?

It's one for the good ol' big noters isn't it?

It comes out of someone who is comparing what they have in their life to others who have less. It's used as a self-convincing trope for people who are absolutely not living their dream but want you to think they are (and that you're probably not). It's used by some people to make you feel bad, and them feel better.

Because, if so few of us are actually living our dream, but we hear from someone else that they are, it's probably going to make us at least a little bit envious of them.

Being a therapist has given me a really interesting perspective on the notion of living the dream. I hear it a lot. During my first session with a new client, they will often start by telling me they don't know why they are even here talking to me – "my life's a dream really", they say.

And with little prompting they then launch into 45 minutes of counter-evidence that tells me (and them) that they are actually not really living the dream right now.

They want to be. So badly. And I get it.

Humans are basically pretty competitive animals. And jealous animals.

When we hear from someone that they are literally living the best life they could have ever dreamed of, but we know that ours isn't quite as shiny and perfect, it's pretty natural to be at least a little envious of that.

Which is why I think this is a crappy bit of advice.

It goes hand in hand with the Instagram highlight reel of most people's life on social media.

I'll show you the good bits. The dream bits.

But the hard stuff? I'll keep that for my therapist.

———————————— . ————————————

That's impossible.

I reckon the majority of times when someone says, 'that's impossible', what they are really saying is 'that's impossible for *me*'.

They are saying 'I give up before I really try'.

And they saying 'you should just give up too'.

As I said before, I am not saying *everything* is possible. Human invisibility or immortality are not possible, regardless of how hard you try.

But plenty of things are achievable, albeit with some difficulty or effort or persistence.

The writer, Paul Hudson[53], believes we can limit ourselves to the point where we don't even try.

"Sometimes we think things as impossible because we're underestimating our cognitive and physical abilities", he writes[54].

"We create impossibilities.

As the creatures who rule the world, we're the ones to blame for limitations on the changes we can make.

---

[53] @MrPaulHudson

[54] https://www.elitedaily.com/life/motivation/its-only-impossible-for-them/1111703

In reality, we're all capable of making huge, positive impacts."

Maybe as adults we need to retain some of the aspiration we have as children. "When we're younger", Hudson writes, before we're taught to believe that things are impossible, we're aware of our potential. We may not be aware of the necessary steps or sacrifices required to make the changes that will lead us to success, but we feel we can accomplish anything we set our minds to.

What happened to those people? Maybe we were young and ignorant; now we're old and dumb.

So many of us have lost hope in a better future, a better life, a more pleasant experience.

We limit ourselves to what we can accomplish.

By doing so, we guarantee the change we're dreaming of never manages to arrive.

If there's a way to fail at life, this is certainly it. If you limit what you can accomplish, what you can experience, and what level of wisdom you can achieve, I guarantee you will get exactly that: a limited experience."

———————————— · ————————————

It is what it is.

The silver medal for the most annoying bit of terrible advice that really gets up my nose is this one.

The reason?

A lot of people use it as a resignation, a sign that they have given up on trying to buck the inevitability of something, and that – at times – it is the signal that we are conforming or quitting to come in line with someone else's story, or someone else's expectations of us.

This advice comes from someone who has given up all hope.

The context is often you wanting something to change. Someone else doesn't think it can change, and eventually they enlist you to support their sense of defeat.

The translation: stop trying.

You can't change anything.

Everything is pre-determined.

We are all useless.

Geez, that's grim.

Instead of 'it is what it is', I try to think in terms of 'it isn't what I want it to be'.

That right now, things might be a certain way, but in the future, I am hoping they will change. That I will change them.

That sounds a hell of a lot more positive and affirming to me.

The writer, Genefe Navilon[55], isn't a fan of the advice either. "It is not a phrase given with empathy", she writes. "In fact, when facing emotional turmoil, many of us would find it dismissive and harsh.

Others would call it is a useless phrase, something you say in defeat. In conversation, it's only a filler to repeat what has already been said.

The American writer, Taylor Maness agrees that is signals our defeat. "This phrase is worrying because it is far more than an autopilot response people use; it is a complete mentality"[56].

That sense of inevitability and the inability to change one's circumstance regardless of what we do or how much we try pervades all of our lives if we allow the phrase to be our motto.

Maness writes that it infers "all situations are concrete and any attempts we make to fix them would be pointless".

---

[55] ideapod.com/author/genefe/

[56] Ninertimes.com

Professor Diane Dreher[57] thinks it can also have a lasting effect on our mental health.

"This is an incredibly destructive mindset to have. We have a basic need to feel a sense of control over what happens in our lives, and deprivation of this need could lead to heightened anxiety and even depression", she writes.

Maness again: "You should not surrender to the notion that you have no say in what happens to you.

The thought that we don't have control over what happens in our lives is both terrifying and mostly untrue.

Yes, we have no control over the weather or what others do.

We do, on the other hand, have complete say in how we react to these circumstances and the actions we will take in response.

Also, many things in life are nowhere near as concreate as we make them out to be.

Many situations are malleable to some extent and can be shaped by our actions. We just have to make the conscious decision to take those actions."

---

[57] www.dianedreher.com

The more a person needs to be right, the less certain he is.

Meir Ezra

Everything happens for a reason.

And the winner is ...

Yes, this is *the* suckiest bit of advice that anyone ever gives.

Everything happens for a reason?

There is a reason why my nephew got cancer when he was six years old?

There is a reason why somebody abused me as a kid?

There is a reason why one child born today will be born into wealth and opulence and opportunity, and another into squalor and poverty and starvation?

Ok then, what is it?

This rubbish sentence is a favourite of anyone who finds themselves in a situation where they don't have to say anything, they can't think of anything to say anyway, but still can't seem to help themselves and have to say something.

Something bad has happened. It's cruel and doesn't make sense.

Person A is searching for an answer and to make sense of the situation.

Person B doesn't have an answer (because there may not be one).

What they are really saying is: "This is hard. I don't know what to say. It might get better though…?"

And even if it could be true that everything happens for a reason, then that also means that everything has been pre-ordained.

That there is no free will.

That we are all playing out lives that have already been written and any changes to which can't be made.

That's bleak.

And it's also … lazy.

The author, Thomas Koulopoulos[58] writes that it's the "same sort of lazy thinking that we buy into when we accept that success is just about being at the right place at the right time.

"Hey, that could have been me if I'd just had the same breaks he did!"

Sure, but apparently the same force that is making everything happen for a reason isn't too keen on giving you a break.

This isn't an assault on faith.

---

[58] @TKSpeaks

I'd actually like to believe that any higher power would prefer granting us free choice over marionette strings".

And that's what makes it resemble another infuriating sentence: "God works in mysterious ways".

So mysterious that none of us can work them out?

What could be the point of that?

Both sentences stifle curiosity.

Instead of encouraging us to seek out the answers as to why something happens or has happened, our acceptance that everything is due to some playbook that's already been written, also stops us searching for any further answers.

These just seem like things people say when they don't understand what is happening and/or they don't know what else to say.

Maybe just say nothing.

Still with me?

I just want to say two things to you right now:

1. Thank you for buying my book in the first place, and then for giving me so much of your attention and time for so long reading this far. I really hope you are getting something positive from it.

and

2. If you *are* getting something positive from it, can you please give the book a review wherever you purchased it, or on social media somewhere?

It would really help me a lot, and help a lot of other people who might also be struggling with either giving too much advice, or getting too much of it.

Thanks,
Nick.

@nickbowditch.   #youradvicesucks

CHAPTER 6:

How to stop

getting advice.

One sure-fire way to reduce the amount of crappy advice circulating around is to stop asking for it, and stop giving it.

Let's start with how to stop getting advice.

Sometimes it's not as easy as saying 'well, OK, I am just not going to get any more advice from people then', because so much advice that's given, was never actually asked for.

I'm not a huge fan of unsolicited advice.

I think it shows a lack of respect, a presumption that you know what's best for someone, and for some reason you just *have* to tell them.

I think it's more critical than helpful.

The psychologist, Elizabeth Scott[59], agrees, but also thinks that unsolicited advice-givers might be doing so as a response to their own trauma and need to be heard.

She writes[60] that when someone is regularly offering unsolicited advice, it might be because they are "driven to do so by a need for emotional validation or personal power.

People who grow up in chronically stressful environments in which they do not feel safe, or in emotionally invalidating environments in which

---

[59] @ elizabethscott

[60] https://www.verywellmind.com/handle-unwanted-advice-with-minimal-stress-3144966

expression of their emotions was punished or ignored, may be self-regulating and seeking to avoid uncomfortable feelings through external validation."

She argues that one way to get this done is by building their sense of self-worth by trying to influence the actions and decisions of others.

It makes them "feel powerful or in control, helping to abate their chronic psychological distress".

However, it's possible that they might also be totally unaware of this.

"These people may also display a problematic degree of emotional vulnerability", Scott writes.

"They become upset very quickly, expressing emotions dramatically, and/or taking a long time to calm down.

It is possible that their emotions were only validated in childhood when they were at their loudest, encouraging them to adopt responses to discomfort that are hyperbolic in most situations".

———————————— · ————————————

Boundaries people!

Humans are not great at boundaries.

Setting them, holding them, or defending them when they are breached.

Regardless of the motivation of the unsolicited advice-giver, for most of us, being good at boundaries is the great antidote against it.

Being able to set a solid boundary and telling the world – verbally or non-verbally – that it's a boundary you intend to hold and any external input isn't actually required, is a really helpful skill to have.

One of the things that make it more difficult for us to hold a boundary against unwanted advice, though, is that the majority of it comes from someone who we have a close relationship with.

A 2016 study[61] showed that people give their friends and close relations unsolicited advice at a very early stage of a supportive interaction around 70% of the time.

We can't help ourselves.

But we can set solid boundaries, and we can defend them if we choose to as well.

---

[61] Feng B, Magen E. (2016). Relationship closeness predicts unsolicited advice giving in supportive interactions. Journal of Social and Personal Relationships, 33(6):751-767.

And we can always decline advice, either politely at first, or less politely if we need to after that.

_____ . _____

The polite decline.

One of the keys for the polite decline is to be able to validate without over-identifying.

"You can let them know that you've heard them and appreciate where they are coming from", Dr. Scott writes, "without taking on the potentially damaging narrative that you couldn't have gotten by without their help.

To do this while proactively communicating a boundary around further advice, you might say something like:

"Thanks for the idea.
I have my own plan for handling this,
but I really appreciate your perspective
and will take it into consideration.
Can I let you know when I need help in the future?"

The psychotherapist Sharon Martin[62], who specialises in working with people on perfectionism, codependence, and people-pleasing, adds that it's

---

[62] https://www.livewellwithsharonmartin.com/

important to consider who the advice-giver is and adjust the politeness of your decline accordingly.

"Your approach will probably depend on who is giving you the advice, about what, and how often", she writes.

"Generally, the best approach is to be direct and polite about what you need or want".

She suggests a few different ways that the decline can happen in a polite way that doesn't necessarily affect your relationship with the advice-giver.

Something like:

"I know you mean well, but I'm not looking for advice. What I'd really like is _____ "

"Right now, I just want to vent. I'm not looking for solutions."

"The most helpful thing you can do
is to sit with me and listen"

or

"I appreciate your ideas, but I
want to figure this out on my own."

Martin again: "You may also want to take preventative measures, especially with routine offenders, and start conversations by letting them know if you're looking for empathy or guidance/feedback.

This can set expectations and help others know how best to support you".

———————————————— · ————————————————

The less polite decline.

Everyone has their limits.

And there might be a need for a less polite, and more forceful decline when unsolicited advice is offered, even when it's from a loved one.

Asserting a boundary can be a difficult thing, especially if you are someone who would rather do anything than feel like you are in a confrontational exchange.

Another challenge is to tread that fine line between asserting yourself strongly and just being a bit passive-aggressive.

Sharon Martin has some suggestions of slightly stronger and less polite ways to decline advice without a hint of passive-aggression.

She suggests starting with something like:

"That doesn't feel like the
right approach for me"

It's comfortable and non-threatening.

But she also suggests something a lot more direct too.

"I know you're trying to help,
but I don't need any more advice."

or

"That's not something I want to discuss."

Or what really should be the last word on the subject:

"I feel inadequate and annoyed when
you repeatedly tell me what to do.
I know you care about me and I'll
let you know when I need help."

———————————————— · ————————————————

Back yourself.

If you take nothing else out of reading this book, I would love you to think about whether you might benefit from backing yourself a bit more.

I'm not saying that the aim should be to never ask for help again in your life, but advice-givers, particularly the unsolicited advice-givers, are pretty adept at picking out people who they feel like they can influence, however benevolently.

There are a few things that I speak to clients and audiences at conferences about that can help with developing a greater sense of self-confidence and self-assuredness.

The first is to ensure that other people's *outer* voice doesn't become our *inner* voice.

What I mean by that is, sometimes we have people in our lives who are, let's face it, not great for us.

They blame us for everything.

They belittle us and reduce our value.

They negatively affect our self-esteem through almost constant negative appraisal.

And sometimes we hear their voice in our head so often, that it starts to instead be *our* voice, and starts to dictate how we feel, and how we talk, about ourselves.

Ensuring that we can hear the difference between someone else's negativity and our own inner strength is a huge factor in us being able to back ourselves and not seek advice so regularly.

The second way is to avoid comparison as much as you can.

We do it largely unconsciously, but comparing ourselves to someone else often doesn't help us grow, it just helps us feel bad about ourselves.

And then the final strategy that helps with our self-confidence and reduces the likelihood of us seeking advice from others is to give up the pursuit of absolute perfection.

As Salvador Dali said, "Have no fear of perfection, you'll never reach it."

Perfectionism is such a happiness-killer.

And not just for the perfectionist themselves.

I prefer not to try to be perfect, I try instead to be valuable.

And if I am consistently adding some value to the world, I am much less likely to be a target of the unsolicited advice-giver.

She generally gave herself very good advice (though she seldom followed it).

Lewis Carroll,
Alice's Adventure in Wonderland

CHAPTER 7:

How to stop
giving advice.

The big
question:
how do we
stop doing
something
that most of
us are unaware
we are doing
in the first place?

So, we've come to here.

We've looked at what advice looks like, how it feels to get it, how to stop asking for it, and I have left probably the most difficult thing until last: how to stop *giving* advice.

It's difficult because, for most of us, we don't know we are giving unsolicited advice, and if we did, we would surely stop doing it.

Try something with me.

When you read each of the next few bits of dialogue, I want you to just try to be mindful of what your initial *instinctive* feeling or action would be. And try to be honest with yourself about it.

Amy:

"John has cheated on me again.
I don't know what to do."

Matt:

"I have been offered a new job at work.
It's more money and more responsibility,
but I don't know whether to take it or not."

Carol:

"My teenage son keeps coming home
late and doesn't listen to me. I keep putting
fuel in his car though."

Pete:

"I really do love her. She wants me to
propose, I know she does. We have been
together for 7 years now. I'm not sure
what to do."

Ok, now *honestly* did you hear any of those bits of dialogue and think you would say to them, "well, what do *you* think you should do?"

Or did you not only quickly formulate an opinion about what they should do, and then get ready to spew it out to them, even though none of them were actually asking for advice?

I'm going to go out on a limb and suggest your response to each of those scenarios was something like this:

To Amy:

"You should dump that idiot.
You're too good for him anyway."

To Matt:

"What??? You should take it!
You've been there for ages and done
the hard work. You'd be stupid
not to take it!"

To Carol:

"Stop putting fuel in his car then!
He's taking the piss, and you are
just enabling his behaviour."

To Pete:

"You're not going to do any better.
What are you waiting for?"

So, there's a couple of problems with those responses.

First, neither Amy, Matt, Carol, or Pete actually asked you for your opinion or your advice on their situations.

Secondly, you don't have all the data. You don't know the dynamics of Amy's relationship with John, or that it's Amy who has cheated repeatedly on John in the past.

You don't know that Matt actually really loves his current position at work and the life-balance he can have in the current job, but will lose if he takes the promotion. You also don't know that he lives with anxiety and a big decision like that, as well as the ensuing responsibility of a higher-up position would be really troublesome for his mental health.

You don't know that Carol's son is working to support himself and contribute to Carol's household and that she really needs his financial input at the moment.

You also don't know that Carol prefers to put fuel in his car so that he drives to work and doesn't get a lift with some of his workmates who are really reckless and drive dangerously.

And you don't know that Pete has been engaged before and it ended really badly.

So badly in fact that he is now really reluctant to go through that kind of trauma again.

You also don't know that Pete is thinking about ending the relationship but doesn't know how to do it without hurting his girlfriend just yet.

And you know what?

You'll *never* know those things now.

And the next time that Amy, Matt, Carol, or Pete want someone to listen to them and not judge them, or – dare I say it – ask someone for advice, you know who they are not going to feel comfortable doing that with?

Yep, you.

OK, so how do you stop giving advice that isn't wanted, particularly when you might not even be aware that you are doing it?

Leave some space.

A really handy skill in this situation is when you feel yourself rushing to give your opinion, give some space instead.

Wait.

See if they were going to add something else.

Let them hear what they have said out loud.

Give yourself some time to consider what you are going to say, or even if you are going to say anything.

Rob Kendall[63] is an expert in the dynamics of effective communication.

He says that when you create a bit of space in that moment, it also gives the other person a chance just to be listened to for a moment.

"More often than not", Kendall writes[64], "someone will raise an issue because they want to be *heard* rather than have it *fixed*.

The extent to which many men tend to do this drives women mad.

---

[63] @Rob_Kendall

[64] https://www.psychologytoday.com/au/blog/blamestorming/201506/why-people-may-not-want-your-advice

But while there is a gender bias toward this habit, it's not exclusive to men; people of both sexes want to be heard.

You can easily test this theory by considering who in your life you speak to when you have a problem, and who you *avoid*.

We tend to go to the people who will give us space rather than opinions."

———————————— . ————————————

"I'm not giving advice, I'm giving information."

If someone doesn't know something, but *I* know something, shouldn't it be OK for me to tell them?

> Well, it depends.

> Mostly on whether they asked you or not.

> But let's assume they asked for a moment.

> Are they asking for advice or information?

> And are you delivering advice or information?

> If you start your information-providing-sentence with:

"I reckon you have got to …"

"Why don't you just …"

"You should …"

"Don't you think that …"

... then there's a pretty good chance you are not giving information, or at least that it won't be heard that way.

———————————————— . ————————————————

Understand your own motivation.

Bringing some of your awareness to why you want (or need) to give advice is a great way to reduce the amount of advice you are dishing out every day.

Is it the need to be heard?

Is it that you are generally *not* heard?

Do you need to be right?

Do you need everyone else to be successful and happy and safe?

Seth Meyers[65] is a Clinical Psychologist and author.

He says that your motivation to give advice might be somewhat out of control and largely due to your personality type.

"People who give a lot of advice tend to have a rigid personality", Dr. Meyers writes[66]. "They can easily become overly concerned with making sure everyone around them is toeing the line, which makes them overbearing and intolerant."

---

[65] @drsethmeyers

[66] https://www.truity.com/blog/why-ntjs-love-give-unsolicited-advice-and-why-thats-bad-everyone

"They have an exaggerated sense of their own competence. They can be critical of others while unwavering in their belief in their own superiority.

They tend to lack awareness. As logical, thinking types, they are uncomfortable with the world of emotion and often brush it aside without considering how their actions affect people or even why they're giving advice.

They seek a sense of control.

When someone shares a difficult situation with them, they want to solve the problem, in part, to relieve themselves of the anxiety they feel when things are in disarray.

Telling someone what to do makes them feel better.

Unfortunately, they tend to overlook how it makes the other person feel."

Meyers believes that people giving unsolicited advice is more about how that makes *them* feel, as opposed to a genuine need to solve another person's problem.

That's rough.

Meyers also adds, though, that this need for advice-givers to have control is largely a subconscious one and comes out of their own self-doubt.

"They constantly seek power because they don't feel powerful", he writes. "

Just giving advice makes them feel important."

OK, so if you are a regular advice-giver, none of that is probably very nice to read.

So, let's turn it into a positive thing.

How can you be more aware of it, and how can you stop dishing out your advice all over the place?

—————————————— · ——————————————

"What do you need from me?"

This is a great place to start.

Knowing what a person needs from you *immediately* removes the need for you to try to decipher what's going on, and the best way to respond to them.

And you know the easiest way to know what someone needs from you?

Ask them.

Consider one of your friends or colleagues sitting at lunch with you comes out, unpromoted, with a sentence something like this:

"Geez, I hate this job.
I don't know how much longer
I can keep coming here
and doing it."

Again, the natural urge might be to step straight in and start delivering sentences that include words like *should*, *must*, and *don't you think*.

But maybe this is the time to say *nothing*.

Something I have learned from engaging clients in therapy for a while now is that when you don't speak, you create a space for them to say more than they had planned to, or get to what they really want to say.

Just listen.

Chances are they will elaborate and all of a sudden you will find yourself in a conversation, rather than a lesson.

When they are finished sharing whatever it is they want to, you will have a much better idea of why they are actually talking to you about this.

Maybe you understand because you are in a similar role.

Maybe you have told them you also hate your job before.

Or maybe they just want to download it out loud to someone, and they trust you.

At this stage, you still don't really know what they want from you, and what role they are casting you in.

So ... ask them.

I have found that one of the most effective ways to move the conversation forward here is to simply ask: "what do you need from me?"

The beauty of this sentence is that it basically has two different responses.

They can either tell you that they don't need anything from you, they just want to tell someone and they just want you to listen. Or, they might ask for some practical suggestions on how to best manage their work situation going forward.

I guarantee you that the majority of people – when actually asked – will say that they would just love someone to listen without lecturing them or giving them advice.

If, on the other hand, they *do* want your input, I usually try to choose from one of these three well-worn sentences.

_____ . _____

"What do *you* think you should do?"

Another version of this one is, "what is your gut telling you?"

People love to be given autonomy over their thoughts and decisions, while also having someone else validate their own opinions as worthwhile and sound.

And this first one does both.

I know it's a bit of a therapist cliché that we always ask clients, "and how does that make you feel?".

But there is a reason why that's a cliché, and it's that it *works*.

It encourages someone to not only search for the feeling they are feeling, but also to say it out loud which brings further awareness to it.

Asking someone "what do you think you should do" is another version of this awareness-seeking kind of question.

Chances are they might already have a really solid opinion on what they should do, but it might be hidden under layers of self-doubt and low self-esteem.

Asking them shines light on it.

It's also another way for the compulsive advice-giver to check themselves and not leap straight in with advice. Pausing for a second and then asking them what they think they should do, if nothing else, slows down your own advice-giving train a bit.

_____ . _____

"I can tell you what *I* would do."

This one might seem like advice, but hear me out.

When I was a participant in group therapy while I was in rehab, the therapists would often stop someone from speaking if they weren't speaking in the 'I'.

This means not giving your own perspective, but rather saying what you think the group – or the world – is thinking or saying about something.

It turns, "You make everyone feel uncomfortable when you say that" to "you make *me* feel uncomfortable when you say that."

And the reason for bringing things back to your own perspective is kind of the whole theme of this book.

You don't know what you don't know, and the only thing we really ever know comes from our own lived experience or perspective.

Instead of shying away from experiencing your own perspective, this prompt helps you lean into it, and lean away from giving advice about something you don't have all the data on.

That's the power of sentences like "I can tell you what I would do" or "I have done this in the past" or "I don't know the whole situation so I can only speak for myself and what I would do".

They in no way say, "and because I feel that and am telling you that, you should also do exactly the same thing".

If anything, it's owning the fact that you don't have all the data *but* you have been in a similar situation, or if you were, then this is what you would feel or say.

It is devoid of judgement.

It is not directive or controlling.

But it's a way to say I have heard what you said, and this is the only way I can relate to that.

———————————— · ————————————

"How can I help?"

The third one is much less open to interpretation by the person you are talking to and who is telling you about their problem.

It says I have heard you and now I am asking you what you would like me to do.

"How can I help?"

Again, this might draw a response of "nothing really, I just want you to listen".

But if they have some way that you can help them in mind, you have invited them to share it.

And if they ask you to do something, or say something, or give an opinion on something, your 'advice' is, at least, coming from them setting the scene and deciding the parameters, as opposed to you just vomiting your advice out on to them.

"Can you help me look
for a new job?"

"Can you come with me when
I speak to our manager?"

"Can you write me a reference
for a new job?"

"Can you keep being my
friend after I quit and we
don't work together anymore?"

None of these responses come out if you just launch into your advice-giving.

How can you help?

By listening.

Asking what they need.

And then listening some more.

CHAPTER 8:

The start.

It's tempting to call the conclusion chapter, 'The End', but I really hope it's not.

When I think about the situations in which I gave people advice that (a) I knew absolutely nothing about really and (b) was never asked for, it's frankly pretty cringe-worthy.

Over the course of my life, I have probably hurt a lot of people with my advice, and with my need to share my advice with them.

I have alienated people and, even though now I'm a reformed advice-giver, they have been lost to my life forever.

It's a huge regret of mine. And one that I hope that you might be able to avoid if you, too, are a compulsive advice-giver.

I talk, and write, a lot about kindness.

I honestly think it's the antidote to so many of the modern world's problems.

But there is nothing kind about the way that I used to spit advice at people, whether they wanted it or not.

And there's everything kind about my new-found skill of listening, holding space, nodding, and saying nothing.

I know now that saying less is saying so much more.

I am sorry if you are one of the people I subjected to my continual flow of advice (mostly probably terrible advice).

I am sorry that I didn't just sit and listen when you probably needed it.

And I'm sorry that I might have lost your wisdom and friendship from my life because of it.

There is kindness in listening.

Thank you for listening to me.